Performance Sailing

STEPHEN COLGATE

Chief Executive Officer, Offshore Sailing School, Ltd.

Illustrations: Joseph Dyas

Copyright © 1993 by Steve Colgate

Published in 1993 by Steve Colgate
Offshore Sailing School, Ltd
16731 McGregor Blvd.
Ft. Myers, FL 33908
800-221-4326

ISBN 0-914747-03-7

CONTENTS

CHAPTER I

CHAPTER II

CHAPTER III

CHAPTER IV

CHAPTER V

FOREWARD

This book is directed to that large portion of the sailing population who have just learned to sail but have no present interest in cruising or racing. It is for those who want to be able to enjoy more thoroughly an afternoon sail on a small open cockpit sailboat — to know what to do in emergencies, to sail the boat at peak performance, to fuss around with navigation for the fun of it, to overcome any fear of flying a spinnaker — in short, to achieve more satisfaction from sailing than ever before.

I have written many articles and chapters for books on the above subjects but never previously compiled these together for the sailor who just wants to improve his or her ability to day-sail. This book is a compilation of past writings along with new subjects. Much of what I cover can be transferred to the race course and this is incorporated in order to improve sailing performance. To sail fast usually means to sail well. Speed means precision of technique. Precision of technique creates self confidence and personal satisfaction.

CHAPTER I

SAILS

SAIL SHAPE

There is probably no other speed determinant so important as a sailboat's sails and the manner in which they are set or trimmed. Keep in mind that sail material is a cloth and is constantly stretching as the forces on it change. The forces change not only when the wind strength changes, but also when the boat slows down as when plowing into waves or speeds up as when surfing or sailing in smooth water. To control this stretch, and thereby the shape of the sail, numerous adjustment devices are used. Before we look at the specific devices, let's discuss the desirable end result.

Sails power a sailboat much like an engine powers a car. When a car is moving slowly, uphill or over a bumpy terrain, you keep it in low (first) gear. As it picks up speed and the ground levels off, you shift to second gear. When the car is moving fast on a smooth road, you shift to high. So with a sailboat. Full sails are the low gear and flat sails are high. When seas are heavy and the boat is sailing slowly ("stop and go" as it hits each wave), the sails need power. Full sails are the answer. In smooth water and high winds when the sailboat is moving its fastest, flat sails are desirable.

DRAFT

The mainsail is a very versatile sail and can be made flat or full at will. But, you may ask, what is a "full sail" or a "flat sail?" The terms are relative. A sail is flatter or fuller than another based on the relationship of the maximum depth of the curvature (the draft) to the distance from luff to leech (the chord). Photo 1 shows the cross-section of a mainsail. An imaginary line drawn from luff to leech is the chord. A line drawn perpendicular to the chord at the point where the sail is the greatest distance from the chord is the "draft" or "camber." The "camber-to-chord ratio" is the relation of this distance to the chord, usually expressed as a percentage. If the chord is 120″ and the draft of camber is 12″ deep, the camber-to-chord ratio is 10 to 1 or 10%. Sails can be used effectively as flat as 5%

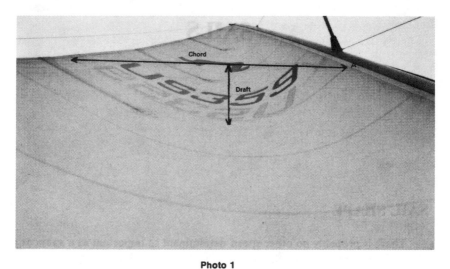

Photo 1
Draft is the maximum depth of the sail measured from the chord –
an imaginary straight line from luff to leech.

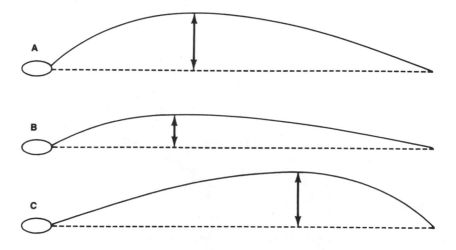

Figure 1
The maximum draft of a sail may be found in numerous locations.

or as full as 20% at the Center of Effort, depending on the class of boat and the sailing conditions. The draft varies at different heights up the sail.

Of even more importance is the position of maximum draft in the sail. Figure 1 shows three sails all with the same camber-to-chord ratio, but with quite different locations of the maximum draft. A has the draft in the desirable location for a mainsail — 40% to 50% aft from the leading edge (the luff). B shows the draft forward, near the mast. This can happen when a sail is designed to accept a certain amount of mast bend, but the sailor doesn't bend the mast enough.

The sailmaker puts draft into the sail in two ways: by a "luff and foot round" and by "broadseaming." If you laid a mainsail on the floor and "luff and foot round" was the only draft producer, it would look like Figure 2. However, when it is put on a straight mast and boom the excess material becomes draft. As the material stretches in the wind, this draft moves aft toward the desired location in

Figure 2
The extra material along the luff and foot of a mainsail become draft when on a straight mast and boom.

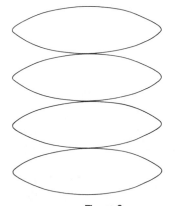

Figure 3
Before it's sewn together, a football may look something like this.

the middle of the sail. In light winds on a straight mast, the draft created by luff round will be forward, near the mast. If you bend the mast and boom to conform with the designed edge round, then the sail will be flat as a board.

The other method of obtaining draft, broadseaming, is simply narrowing the panels of cloth before they are stitched together. To understand how this creates draft, imagine a football that has been taken apart. It looks somewhat like Figure 3. Sewn together, it becomes a football. The same method is practiced in sailmaking as in Figure 4. Draft created in this manner is placed exactly where the sailmaker wants it and does not depend on mast bend or stretch to place its location. A combination of both methods is used in the manufacture of all sails.

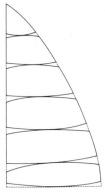

Figure 4

A sailmaker also gets draft by curving the panels and then sewing them together.

C in Figure 1 shows the maximum draft aft, near the leech of the mainsail. As the breeze freshens, sail material stretches and the draft tends to move aft toward the leech. This movement will cause the battens to cock to windward in the mainsail and produce a less efficient airfoil. Increased tension on the luff can keep this movement to a minimum.

SAIL CONSTRUCTION

But first, just a bit about how a sail is constructed. The threads that run across a panel of sailcloth are called the filling threads, otherwise known as the "weft" (pronounced "woof") or the "fill." The threads that run lengthwise are called the "warp." Warp stretches more than weft, but the greatest stretch comes in a diagonal direction, called the "bias." Most sails are designed with this stretch in mind.

For example, the mainsheet will exert the greatest force on a mainsail, and most of it will fall on the leech. Consequently, the panels of cloth are sewn together so that the crosswise threads, or filling threads, lie along the leech of the sail (see Figure 5).

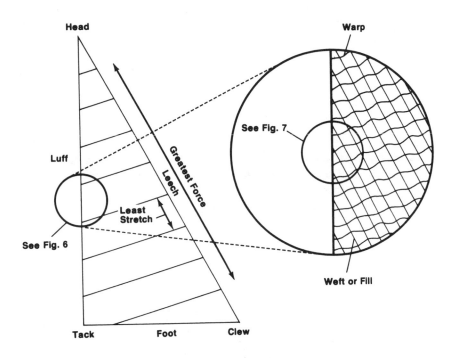

Figure 5
Panels meet the mast on a bias.

Figure 6
*The threads form little diamonds
near the mast.*

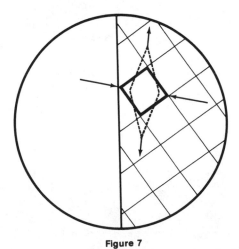

Figure 7
*As the top and bottom of the diamonds are stretched, material is
pulled in from the middle of the sail.*

This means that all the panels along the luff of the sail must be cut on the bias, where stretch is greatest. If we were to blow up a small section of the sail along the mast, we would see that the threads look like a whole bunch of little diamonds at the bias (Figure 6). As we pull down on the luff and increase the tension, each diamond elongates (the dotted lines) and pulls material in from the center of the sail (see Figure 7). If we pull down hard on the luff when there is not enough wind to warrant it, vertical troughs or creases will appear, running parallel to the mast (see Photo 2).

You can simulate this effect by taking a handkerchief and pulling it at two diagonally opposite corners, as in Photo 3. The same troughs will appear just as they will when there is too much luff tension. Photo 4 shows that as the corners are stretched apart on the bias, the material moves upward. The lower corner was even with the instructor's waist and is now a few inches higher.

Photo 2
Excessive luff tension causes wrinkles near the mast.

Photo 3
Hold handkerchief at two corners on the bias.

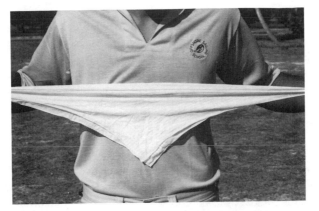

Photo 4
Pull out and creases appear as bottom corner pulls up.

PROPER MAINSAIL ADJUSTMENT

Tensioning the Luff

There are two ways to tension a mainsail's luff — with a downhaul and with a cunningham. In the days of cotton sails, you would buy a sail that was actually too small in light air. This would allow you to stretch it to flatten the sail when the wind velocity increased. Of course, this meant that you would automatically penalize yourself in light air by having reduced sail area.

To solve this little dilemma, Briggs Cunningham, skipper of *Columbia,* winner of the 1958 America's Cup, chose the simple expedient of placing a grommet above the mainsail tack fitting in a full-sized sail. When the sliding gooseneck was pulled by the downhaul as far as possible on the mast and the luff of the sail was stretched as far as it could be, a block and tackle arrangement was attached to a hook running through the grommet. Tightening it added further tension to the luff. Though some wrinkles do appear along the foot below the grommet when the cunningham is in use, they don't seem to make an appreciable difference in the efficiency of the sail. So just forget them.

This grommeted hole in the mainsail has become known as a "cunningham hole" and it is now commonplace in most classes of sailboats. With a cunningham, a sail can be made full-sized for light air performance and still be tensioned along the luff to keep the draft from moving aft when the breeze increases.

A variation of the cunningham is also used on jibs. Many small boats have a cloth tension device attached to the jib near the tack, and a wire that leads to the cockpit can be adjusted to increase or decrease the tension of the luff. The theory is the same for both a jib and a main. But the jib is much more sensitive to luff tension than is the main.

When sailing to windward, the point of maximum draft on a jib should be about 35% of the chord behind the luff, compared to about 50% of the chord in a mainsail. If the wind increases, it's far easier for the draft of a jib to work aft of its normal location, which means you must constantly change the jib luff tension for highest efficiency whenever the wind velocity changes.

Luff tension must also be changed depending upon what point of sail the boat is on. When reaching or running, you want a very full sail with the draft well aft. You should ease off the downhaul and cunningham, in this situation.

The Traveler

An important mainsail adjustment is the traveler — a track with a sliding mainsheet block which runs across the boat beneath the main boom. Travelers with ball bearing cars are preferable because, when close-hauled, those without ball bearings have a tendency to stick (create more friction) under the pressure of the mainsheet.

The traveler's function is to allow the angle of the boom relative to the centerline of the boat to change without allowing the boom to rise. If instead of

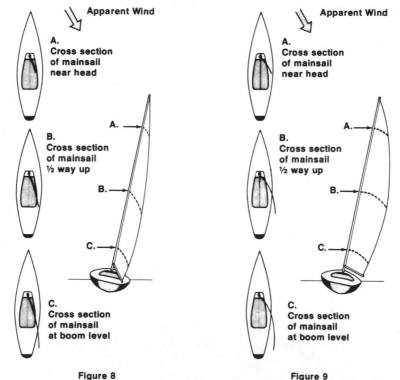

Figure 8	Figure 9
With the mainsheet trimmed tightly, the sail near the top of the mast is at the same angle to the wind as the bottom.	*When the mainsheet is eased, the top part of the sail falls off to leeward.*

using a traveler we ease the mainsheet, the force of the wind on the sail will lift the boom in the air and the top part of the leech will fall off to leeward.

Figure 8 shows the constant angle the apparent wind makes with the luff of the sail over its full length when the mainsheet is trimmed in tight. Figure 9 shows how this angle changes in the upper part of the sail when the mainsheet is eased. The upper part can actually be luffing even though the bottom part is full of air. This effect is called "twist" and is usually undesirable.

There are a couple of exceptions. The wind on the surface of the water is slowed down by friction, so the wind at the top of the mast has a greater velocity than at deck level. Thus, the top of the sail is sailing in a continual puff relative to the bottom of the sail. Apparent wind comes aft in a puff. In order for the apparent wind to have the same angle to the luff all the way up and down, a slight twist at the head of the sail is necessary.

The other exception to the harmful effects of twist is when there is very heavy air. The upper part of the sail greatly affects a boat's heeling, just as weight at the top of the mast does. If you want to reduce heeling, simply reduce the effectiveness of the upper part of the sail by inducing twist. Instead of easing the traveler out, ease the mainsheet.

The traveler is also used to help control heeling. We all know that as a sailboat turns from close-hauled to a reach, one should ease the sails (see Figure 10a). If you don't, the boat will heel way over as the wind hits the windward side of the sail at right angles to it. Forward drive will be reduced because of the lack of drive-producing airflow over the lee side of the sail (Figure 10b). We know that if sails are trimmed properly for a reach, the boat heels less than it does when close-hauled because the drive from the sails is more in the direction of the boat's heading, and heeling force is reduced (Figure 10c).

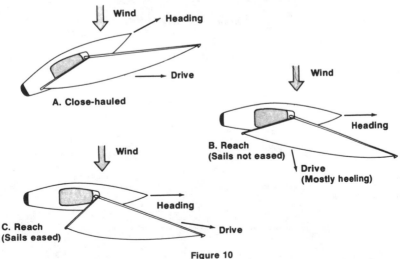

Figure 10

Heeling is reduced when drive and heading line up together.

If we are heeling excessively when close-hauled, we can reduce the heeling by easing the traveler. Many good small boat sailors use the traveler rather than the mainsheet to adjust to changes in wind velocity. Every novice has learned that when you are hit by a puff, you ease the mainsheet and head up into the wind to reduce heeling and avoid a capsize. The advanced sailor does much the same thing, but eases the traveler instead, though this depends to an extent on the type of sailboat. Since the apparent wind comes aft in a puff, easing the traveler maintains the angle the apparent wind makes with the luff of the sail.

As you fall off to a true reach, easing the traveler acts like a boom vang, keeps the boom from rising, and reduces twist. However, its effectiveness ends when the traveler car reaches the outboard end of the track, and the mainsail must go out still further. Now the mainsheet, instead of pulling down, is angled out over the water and a boom vang has to do the work of keeping twist out of the sail. In Photo 5 the vang is not in use and the sail is badly twisted. Photo 6 shows

Photo 5
No vang tension, mainsail twisted so top part is useless.

Photo 6
Vang tight, mainsail presents its full area to the wind.

the difference in the leech when the boom vang is pulled tight. The farther forward in the boat the traveler is located the farther out the boom can go before the traveler car reaches the end of the track and the vang must take over. The closer the traveler is to the boom, the more positive is its control. If the traveler is mounted way down on the cockpit floor a number of feet beneath the boom, a puff may cause the mainsheet to stretch. The boom will lift and move outboard, negating some of the traveler's usefulness.

There is one other use of the traveler. You can trim the main boom up to the centerline of the boat without pulling down hard on the mainsheet. The closer the boom comes to the center of the boat, the higher you can theoretically point. On a light day, however, trimming the main tight can result in a very tight leech. The solution is to leave the mainsheet lightly trimmed and pull the traveler car up to windward, bringing the boom toward the middle of the boat without pulling it down at the same time, as in Photo 7. Now let's look at the backstay.

Photo 7

Pull the traveler car to windward to get the boom near the center without pulling hard on the mainsheet.

The Backstay

The adjustable backstay is a mast bending device. On small boats, a block-and-tackle arrangement is attached to the lower end of the backstay and produces the leverage for bending the mast with a minimum of effort. Other factors are involved in mast bend such as leech tension, angle and length of the spreaders, placement of the partners where the mast goes through the deck (if any), tension on the jumpers (if any), location of the mainsheet blocks along the boom, etc. But for now let's just analyze the backstay. Tightening the backstay bends the mast and flattens the mainsail.

When the backstay is tensioned, the middle of the mast bows forward, lengthening the chord, as the dotted lines in Figure 11 indicate, and decreasing the draft. With a longer chord distance and the same amount of sailcloth as

Figure 11
*Bending the mast changes the camber to chord ratio and flattens
the sail.*

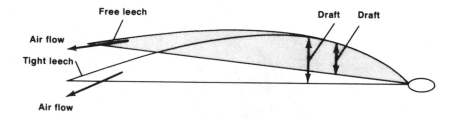

Figure 12
A full leech creates a flatter sail than a tight leech.

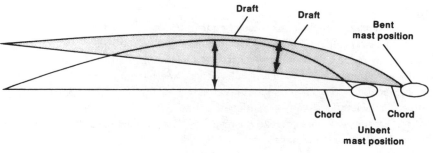

Figure 13
*The combination of moving the mast forward and freeing the leech
really flattens the sail.*

before, the draft has to be less as the excess material built by the sailmakers into the sail along the luff is stretched out and the sail flattened. But also note the action at the top of the mast. It is pulled back and down, which effectively shortens the distance between the top of the mast and the end of the boom. The distance A to B_2 is shorter than the distance A to B_1. This frees the leech of the sail because the material sags off rather than being pulled tight. The end result is indicated by the shaded area in Figure 12. Even if the chord length remains the same, a free leech creates a flatter sail since the draft is less. Figure 12 also shows that the drive will be in a more forward direction, which reduces heeling.

Weather helm is reduced as the leech is freed. With a tight leech, airflow on the windward side of the sail is bent around until it exits off the leech in a windward direction. The tight leech acts like a rudder, forcing the stern to leeward and creating weather helm. But when the leech is freed, the air can flow straight aft or slightly to leeward, which minimizes turning effect of the leech. Figure 13 shows how the combination of the mast moving forward and a freer leech creates a much flatter sail.

The Mainsheet

Mainsheet tension, particularly on light days, will harden up the leech and cock the battens to windward. The sail will look much like the unbent mast position in Figure 13. Photo 8 shows a cocked leech on the boat to the left caused by over-trimming the mainsheet. Because this is a fuller shape, we can say that mainsheet tension makes any cross section of the sail fuller, whereas an eased mainsheet, and the corresponding twist in the sail as the boom rises, makes the cross section of the sail flatter.

Photo 8
On the left, too much mainsheet tension cups the leech of the mainsail.

The Outhaul

The outhaul mainly affects the draft in the lower part of the sail near the boom. Figure 14 shows the outhaul eased, and it is obvious that it creates a greater draft in the sail. Even if the actual draft remains the same, the shortening of the chord makes the camber-to-chord ratio larger, thereby making the sail fuller. Easing the outhaul excessively will cause wrinkles along the foot of the mainsail, as in Photo 9.

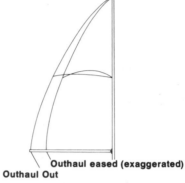

Outhaul eased (exaggerated)
Outhaul Out

Figure 14
An eased outhaul creates a fuller sail.

Photo 9
Easing the outhaul can cause undesirable wrinkles.

HOW TO "SEE" SAIL SHAPE

It's difficult for many sailors to see fine adjustments in sail shape so it's best to use visual aids. In order to determine how much mast bend you have, with an indelible pen draw short vertical lines on the mainsail at spreader height, evenly spaced about three inches apart. Sight up from under the gooseneck to the masthead and determine where an imaginary straight line would fall. With this method we can determine that the mast in Figure 15 has about 13 inches of mast bend.

To see how much twist the mainsail has, sight up the sail from under the boom and line up the top batten with the boom. It should be parallel or falling off a little, but should not be cocked to weather. If there is room to stand on the afterdeck behind the main boom, one can obtain a good overall perspective of the mainsail from that position.

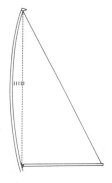

Figure 15

The amount of mast bend can be determined by sighting up the mast past marks placed at known intervals.

Colored tape can be placed on the backstay in small boats to correspond with a certain amount of mast bend. Colored marks on the mainsheet can give you a guide as to how much twist there is in the mainsail leech for given wind conditions. Marks next to the traveler at one-inch increments can help you duplicate the traveler car position. Also, a mark on the jib halyard against a series of marks spaced at equal intervals on the mast can be helpful in duplicating luff tension.

The jib is a little harder to judge. When it is a genoa, overlapping outside the spreader, use the spreader tip as a guideline. Depending on the type of genoa, the lateral jib lead placement, the wind and sea conditions, and the luff tension, the cloth should be trimmed anywhere from a point a few inches off the spreader tips to just touching them. Many sailmakers put a "fast stripe" on genoas. This is a dark stripe midway up the genoa parallel to the deck that makes the draft in the sail very easy to see.

If the jib does not overlap the spreaders the leech will probably point right at them. Place a piece of tape on the spreaders as a guideline and trim the sail until the leech points at the tape.

One way of knowing whether the jib is trimmed in too tight or the draft is too far aft is to observe the amount of backwind in the mainsail. If the backwind extends further back than usual, it is probably caused by overtrimming the jib.

Last, for an overall look at the jib shape, go to the bow and look at the leeward side. This can help you see if the draft has been blown aft.

All the above helps you to duplicate the same shape at another time, but only testing alongside another sailboat will tell you which shape or which sail is fastest. Sailmakers do this all the time when testing sails, so it can help you too if you can find a willing collaborator with a boat equal to yours. Sail side by side close-hauled, each with clear air, keeping one boat as a "control" (don't change anything on it) and changing only one variable (such as the mainsheet tension or mast bend) on the other at any one time.

PROPER JIB ADJUSTMENT

Twist in the mainsail results from the top part of the sail falling off to leeward because of inadequate leech tension. The same problem exists with the jib. Two things determine how much twist a jib will have when beating: jib sheet tension and the fore and aft placement of the jib leads. If the lead is too far aft, the jib sheet will pull along the foot of the sail but there won't be enough downward tension on the leech. The result is that the top part of the sail will tend to luff first.

However, other things can have the same effect as moving the jib lead block forward or aft. For instance, if the mast is raked (leaned) aft by lengthening the jibstay (see Figure 16) it effectively moves the head of the sail aft and the clew is lowered. If the jib lead remains in the same place, raking the mast frees the leech of the jib.

A good rule of thumb is the opening or slot between the jib leech and the body of the mainsail should remain parallel. This means if we induce twist in the mainsail in heavy weather to reduce drive in the upper part of the main, thereby reducing heeling, we must also do the same to the jib.

Figure 16
Raking the mast aft frees the leech of the jib. Move lead forward to maintain leech tension.

Figure 17

As the sheet is eased, the clew goes forward, the sheet angle is lowered, the effective lead goes aft, and twist develops.

Figure 18

As the jib halyard is tensioned, move the lead aft.

Figure 19

As the jib downhaul is tensioned, move the lead forward.

In light air, any fullness should be down low in the jib. You can accomplish
this by easing the jib sheet. This has the same effect as easing the outhaul on the
main along the boom. Easing the jib sheet increases draft by shortening the
distance between the tack and the clew, and this gives you greater drive in light
airs and lumpy seas. However, there is one detrimental side effect to easing the
sheet. As the clew goes out, the angle of the jib sheet is lowered and frees the
leech (see Figure 17). Therefore, to regain the proper leech tension, you must
move the jib lead forward.

The jib tack, jib halyard tension, and jib downhaul, or cunningham, also
affect the location of the clew and the jib lead. One usually increases the tension
on the luff of the sail to control the jib's shape as the wind increases. As the jib
stretches under the force of the increased wind velocity, the draft tends to move
aft in the sail, and more luff tension is required to keep the draft in the same
location. But when the luff tension is increased by tightening the jib halyard,
pulling the head of the sail higher, the clew is lifted higher also, and the lead will
need to be placed further aft (see Figure 18). In heavy air you may even want a
little twist in the sail, and the lead may need to come back even further.

However, if you get your luff tension by pulling down the luff downhaul or
jib cunningham, the clew will be lowered and the lead will appear to be aft of its
previous location (see Figure 19). Since the wind is blowing relatively hard when
this is done, you may not want to change the jib lead position. It is now
effectively aft of where it had been and may produce the desired twist.

Observe what jib halyard tension does to the leech of the sail. As draft is
pulled forward, the leech should become free and flatter. On high aspect sails
(those that are tall and narrow rather than wide and squat), the opposite can
sometimes happen. The halyard pulls on the leech almost as much as on the luff,
because the angle is about the same, so luff tension cups the leech instead of
freeing it.

As a boat falls off onto a reach, the jib sheet is eased and a great deal of twist
can develop. In order to correct this, the lead must go forward again. In the old
days, sailboats did not have effective boom vangs for their mains and the top part
of the mainsail twisted off to leeward when reaching. In order to make the jib
leech match the curve of the main, sailors would move the jib lead aft.

Not so, today. Effective boom vangs keep twist in the main to a minimum
and therefore, little twist is needed in the jib. So in most cases, the lead when on a
reach should go forward, not aft, to pull down on the leech and reduce twist.

One other sensitive adjustment for the jib lead is its correct distance outboard from the centerline of the boat. To find this point, first draw a line from the
tack of the jib to the jib lead and measure the angle it makes with the centerline of
the boat. This is called the "jib lead angle," and it will vary greatly from boat to
boat.

A narrow keelboat will get away with having the jib lead fairly well inboard
and still maintain speed while pointing high. A beamy centerboarder, though,

will have her jib leads further outboard in order to obtain enough drive to go through the seas.

Think of the lateral placement of the jib lead in the same terms as the mainsheet traveler. If the traveler needs to be eased, the jib lead should probably be eased outboard too. The best way to tell whether your jib lead angle is correct is to test your boat against another. Sail close-hauled alongside another boat of the same class and vary the lateral position in or out. The correct location will slow up in increased speed.

You can measure the angle by using the table and diagram in Figure 20. To do so, first measure along the centerline from the tack fitting to any point just forward of the mast (distance AB on the diagram). From B, measure at right angles to the point that intersects a straight line running from the tack fitting to the jib lead (distance BC). Divide BC by AB and carry it to four places. Then consult the table for the jib lead angle in degrees. Example: AB is 59″ and BC is 11″. Eleven divided by 59 is .1864, which is a hair over 10½° in the table.

Start at about 9° on your boat and, in light air, come inboard with light jib sheet tension to about 8°. In heavy air you may be able to go outboard to 11° or even 12° with success. But remember — these adjustments always vary with boat type and the wind and sea conditions.

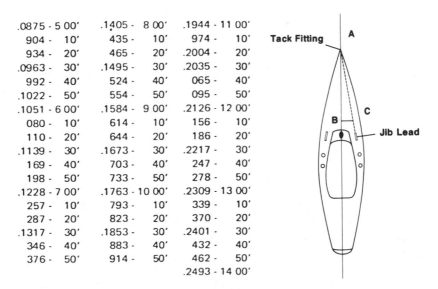

.0875	5 00′	.1405	8 00′	.1944	11 00′
904	10′	435	10′	974	10′
934	20′	465	20′	.2004	20′
.0963	30′	.1495	30′	.2035	30′
992	40′	524	40′	065	40′
.1022	50′	554	50′	095	50′
.1051	6 00′	.1584	9 00′	.2126	12 00′
080	10′	614	10′	156	10′
110	20′	644	20′	186	20′
.1139	30′	.1673	30′	.2217	30′
169	40′	703	40′	247	40′
198	50′	733	50′	278	50′
.1228	7 00′	.1763	10 00′	.2309	13 00′
257	10′	793	10′	339	10′
287	20′	823	20′	370	20′
.1317	30′	.1853	30′	.2401	30′
346	40′	883	40′	432	40′
376	50′	914	50′	462	50′
				.2493	14 00′

Tack Fitting — A — B — C — Jib Lead

Figure 20

Use this table to determine jib-lead angle.

CHAPTER II

BOAT HANDLING

HEELING

Many sailors are very uncomfortable at first when a sailboat heels. One reason is that we are used to a world that stays level and it is unnatural to function properly with the horizon constantly at an angle. Heeling is of such great concern to new sailors that when I recently queried dealers on what question prospective first-time sailboat buyers ask most, the overwhelming response was, "How tippy is it?"

This fear is reinforced by news photographs of capsized sailboats, or of racing crews hiked way out in an apparent effort to keep the boat from tipping over. If the novice steps aboard a small conterboarder at a dock, he is further convinced that all boats are tippy and it will take a crew having the muscles of a gorilla and the agility of a cat to sail them.

Of course, this is just not so. The first time I sailed a Finn dinghy I was scared to death that I'd capsize and make a fool of myself. Motionless in the water, dinghies are very tippy. But the minute they pick up speed they become quite stable. It is not even necessary to hike out. You can sail along quite comfortably just sitting upright on the windward side of the boat, though the boat will heel more and therefore sail more slowly.

The reason racing sailors hike out is not for survival or to keep from capsizing, but to sail the boat more upright and therefore more efficiently. The less heel a sailboat has the more sail area is exposed to the wind and the more quickly it can go. A boat heels in the first place because a keel or centerboard down in the water counteracts the tendency of the boat to be pushed sideways by the wind in the sails (making leeway). Because the keel resists leeway, the side force from the sails up above results in heeling. The more heeling, the more the keel is angled and the less lateral resistance it has. In other words greater heeling creates greater leeway.

21

A boat with a heavy keel can usually resist the heeling force better. However, the heavier the keel the stronger a boat must be built, and the more it probably will weigh. A heavy boat sits deep in the water and pushes a greater volume of water aside when sailing. This increased resistance often can more than offset the increased speed obtained from the greater sail area.

Hull shape also affects heeling. As the sails fill on a tack, one side of the boat sinks into the water and the other side lifts out. When the crew sits on the high side of a wide hull lifting out of the water, he or she obtains more leverage to resist heeling than with a narrow hull. However, another trade-off is involved. The wide hull usually has more wetted surface (square feet of area in contact with the water), and, therefore, more skin friction to slow the boat down when it isn't heeling. Moreover, it doesn't usually sail upwind quite as well, or point as high, as a narrow boat. Because of all these compromises, a wide variety of sailboat designs is available on the market. Racing sailors consider speed above all else; cruising sailors tend to look for comfort, room and ease of handling first. But no matter whether a boat is a beamy centerboarder or a narrow keelboat, the reaction to heeling is predictable and a skipper must make adjustments accordingly.

The one universal effect from heeling is weather helm, and small amounts of it are desirable. Weather helm does give the boat more feel. Instead of having to steer the boat in both directions, you only have to steer it away from the wind because the boat always wants to turn toward the wind. With a slight constant pull of the tiller to windward, you can counteract this tendency of the boat to wander and you can therefore steer the boat in a straight line quite easily.

And with a slight amount of weather helm, the boat will automatically head up in puffs. This reduces heeling and maintains the angle the wind originally made with the sails because the apparent wind (the wind that is blowing on the sails) moves aft from the bow as the wind increases in a puff.

The close-hauled weather helm angle the rudder makes with the water is shown in Figure 21. We are looking down from above and imagining that the

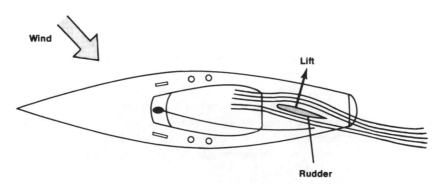

Figure 21
The rudder helps to reduce leeway by producing lift.

rudder can be seen through the boat. Note that the water flow over the rudder is like that of an airfoil. There is lift to windward when the rudder is at the angle in the diagram, but as you can imagine, there is an undesirable pull to leeward whenever the tiller is put to the other side of the boat's centerline.

There are two reasons heeling causes weather helm. First, the shape of the hull on the leeward (curved) side of the bow forces the bow to windward when it's heeled. If you throw a curved piece of wood in the water it doesn't travel in a straight line. Neither does the leeward side of a sailboat when most of the windward side is out of the water. Note the bow wave of the narrow keelboat in Photo 10. The bow wave is much larger on the lee side and this is forcing the bow to weather. The greater the heel, the more pronounced this becomes. Without any heeling, neither bow wave has a chance to overpower the other.

The second reason heeling causes weather helm is that it places the sail area out over the water. In photo 10, if you draw a vertical straight line from the

Photo 10
Large bow wave on leeward side pushes the bow to weather (towards the wind).

Photo 11
Turbulence incidates a stalled rudder resulting from excessive heeling.

leeward edge of the hull you can see that a large portion of sail is not over the boat. The forward pull the sail exerts is therefore out of alignment with the drag of the hull in the water, and this causes a turning moment to windward.

When heeling is excessive, weather helm becomes quite strong. Photo 11 shows a keelboat that is heeled way over. The rudder is being turned to counteract the resulting weather helm but is practically stalled. Also note the turbulence the rudder creates in the left of the photo. There is so much rudder drag here, the boat speed just has to be markedly slower. And, as the boat heels, the rudder comes farther out of the water and loses its effectiveness.

Excessive heeling, therefore, creates weather helm and makes sailing uncomfortable for the crew, tiring for the helmsman who is always pulling hard on the tiller, and inefficient in terms of speed.

TACKING

Now let's look at some of the basic procedures such as tacking and jibing. Most people consider these two maneuvers to be quite simple and they are. However, good sailors refine them to an art form. I'll never forget seeing the great Danish Olympian, Paul Elvstrom, tack a Soling a number of times during a race in gusty, twenty knot winds. The smoothness of each turn was exceptional as the mast described a smooth arc from a constant angle on one tack to the identical angle on the other tack. This is what differentiates the good sailor from the beginner or experienced poor sailor.

By adjusting sail trim and steering angle the mast stays at a constant angle to the water through gusts and lulls in the wind, and crests and troughs of the waves. The boat is not turned too far after a tack (which would cause it to heel over) nor too short causing the boat to stand upright. Also, in a proper tack the boat doesn't heel over just before a tack — a constant problem with new sailors.

For some unfathomable reason, some sailors pull the tiller towards them just before they tack causing the boat to head off and heel over. This causes a strong weather helm, so when the tiller is put to leeward and the boat allowed to tack, it spins quickly into the wind. The speed of the tack sometimes catches the jib sheet crew unawares and the jib backs before it can be released. This forces the boat over on the other tack past 90° causing it to heel badly. At about this point, as the helmsman is trying to steer the boat back up to a close-hauled course on the new tack, the jib finally gets released and is flapping madly. With the jib no longer holding the boat down and the mainsail and the helmsman trying to force the boat up towards the wind, suddenly the boat spins to windward. Just as the crew gets the jib trimmed in on the new side, the boat is pointing so close to the wind that the jib backs again and the whole process is repeated. On top of this, some helmsmen don't sit in a proper comfortable manner and when the boat heels over on the new tack because of the backed jib, they slide to leeward pushing the tiller as they go. With the helm "Hard Alee" they accidently tack again.

On a small boat with a tiller, the proper steps are as follows: the helmsman should make sure he or she is in a comfortable position with their rear end over the edge of the deck. By hooking a leg under a hiking strap or the afterdeck, they can't fall out of the boat, but neither can they slide in if they're over the edge. Once you become accustomed to balancing on the lip of the deck where it joins the topsides, you will never go back to sitting on top of the deck when the boat is heeled.

The jib crew should take the leeward sheet out of its cam cleat so it can be readily released. The windward sheet should be wrapped two or three times around the winch and the slack taken out of it.

The helmsman then allows the natural weather helm of the boat to initiate the tack. In lighter air the crew may lean in to allow the boat to heel more and accentuate the weather helm and in very light air the helmsman may head off just lightly to increase the weather helm. Then, as the boat turns into the wind, and the jib barely starts to luff, the crew releases the jib. This helps continue the turn because the mainsail heads the boat into the wind. The helmsman by this point is steering the boat through the wind.

The reason for initially allowing the boat to turn itself is two fold. First, any strong rudder movement tends to slow the boat down by creating turbulent water flow over the rudder. Second, as the boat turns the rudder follows the original water flow for awhile. The stern doesn't follow the same arc as the bow because the center of rotation is near the middle of the boat. You can see this clearly in a calm harbor with no sails up and nobody holding the tiller. If you shove the bow to port, the stern goes to starboard and the tiller goes to starboard just as if you were on the port tack and were turning the boat into the wind. Since the rudder is following the water flow past the stern, it is obvious that in the beginning of the turn there is little or no drag caused by the tiller going to leeward.

The helmsman, on the starboard tack, is steering with his or her left hand using the tiller extension. As the boat turns and the tiller goes to leeward, the left arm extends. The helmsman then comes into the cockpit swings the tiller extension aft and crosses in front of the tiller, facing forward, with the left arm behind the back. As the helmsman gets over to the new windward side, he or she shifts to the right hand grasping the tiller extension and hikes out.

Meanwhile the crew has also shifted over to the new windward side. This shift of crew weight is sometimes delayed in order to tack faster through a maneuver called "roll tacking." The theory is similar to trying to fly a kite on a windless day. As long as you are running with the kite string pulling the kite, it will rise up in the air. The forward movement creates a breeze and, in turn, this creates lift. When you stop running, the kite falls. Therefore, if we can swing the mast and the sails into the wind, they will stay full and create lift even if there is little or no actual wind. So as the boat turns the crew hikes out hard swinging the mast and sails up over them. The sails stay full of air even though the bow has passed through the eye of the wind. The crew then leaps across the boat and hikes out hard on the new windward side swinging the mast back up towards the wind as the boat settles down on the new tack. Thus, the sails luff only for an instant instead of throughout the whole tack. Roll tacking is an extremely effective maneuver on small dinghies, but also works well on boats as large as Solings, but be sure to check the racing rules about it if you are racing.

JIBING

Jibing without a spinnaker is a fairly simple process. The helmsman should bear off downwind until by-the-lee, watching carefully to avoid jibing accidently. Then, after the proper commands, he or she initiates the jibe. The crew grabs all the parts of the mainsheet and pulls the main boom across. In light air another crew member may pull on the boom vang to help the boom across. Just as the boom passes the centerline of the boat, the helmsman heads back downwind by pulling the tiller to the new windward side. This should negate the tendency for the boat to round up into the wind after a jibe. Even though the rudder is turned, the boat should sail straight. There are two reasons to pull all the parts of the mainsheet at once. First, the mainsail comes in four times faster (if the mainsheet is a four-to-one tackle). In light air this gives the boat a scoot forward, because it's like "pumping" which is explained later. Second, if you pull the line through all the blocks, their friction reduces the speed with which the mainsheet may be eased on the new side after the boom crosses the centerline. This, in turn, increases the wind power in the sail and enhances the tendency for the boat to round up into the wind, to broach. As in tacking, the helmsman should face forward at all times.

LIGHT AIR SAILING

It has long been thought that one should have flat sails in heavy air and full sails in light air. However, most top sailors in the country have come to recognize that a full sail is needed only when power is required, no matter whether the wind is light or heavy. In drifting conditions, it is conceded by most that one needs a flat sail.

When there is practically no wind, sails have to be set to maximize fully any puff that comes along. If there is a deep curvature in the sail, a puff is unable to attach itself readily to the lee side of the sail, since the airflow has to make too large a turn. A flat sail is, therefore, desirable in such conditions, for it doesn't require the air to deflect far from its normal direction to attach to the sail.

As soon as there's a breeze of 2 or 3 knots, full sails are required for low-speed power and acceleration. The racing sailor will start flattening the sails again at 10 or 12 knots of wind speed. A small sailboat that uses crew weight to stay flat may need to flatten sails earlier. A heavy keelboat sailing in heavy seas may need full sails up to a higher wind velocity. It all depends on the boat, the crew, and the wind and sea conditions.

In light air conditions, be careful not to over bend the mast or you will "turn the sail inside out." This occurs when the mast is bent more than the amount of luff roach that has been built into the sail. The visual result will be obvious by the wrinkles emanating from the clew (see Photo 12).

In purely drifting conditions, the cunningham and the main boom downhaul should not be tensioned. Both tend to pull the position of maximum draft forward, but neither one will flatten the sail. If you pull down hard on the cunningham in light air, the draft will go all the way forward and form a cup along with mast. Any puff hitting the sail is unable to make such a sharp bend, and will fail to produce adequate airflow to produce lift. However, you want to avoid the wrinkles near the mast, shown in Photo 13, caused by no luff tension at all.

In drifting conditions, in addition to having flat sails and light trim, you also must trim the sails as if you were close reaching. The boom, for example, never should be over the centerline of the boat because if a zephyr does hit the sail, the

Photo 12

Wrinkles from the clew to the mast indicate the mast is over bent.

Photo 13

The small wrinkles along the luff can be cured by tightening the cunningham. Straighten the mast a little to cure the large wrinkles from the clew.

force is translated into leeway rather than forward motion. The jib should be led further outboard than when there is a breeze. In light air you cannot ''strap'' the sails in. Doing so just slows the boat down.

The jib is played much the same way as the main in light air. A jib should have very light halyard and sheet tension, and little to no luff tension. In some cases, the jib sheet should be hand-held so its weight doesn't tighten or collapse the jib leech. A jib is shaped so that the clew is aft of a point directly below the head. When there is no wind to fill the sail, gravity causes the heavy clew to fall forward directly beneath the head. This cups the foot of the sail and tightens the leech. The effect is similar to releasing the outhaul of the main boom (see Figure 14). Holding the clew by hand will keep it from drooping forward.

One of the most important things to remember is that once you can get a sailboat moving, its mass tends to keep it going even if the wind dies for a moment or two. Furthermore, as the boat moves, it creates an increased amount of apparent wind just by its own movement through the water. The cumulative effect of a little speed is amazing. Some large close-winded boats like 12-Meters can sail extraordinarily fast in practically no wind at all.

But there are a number of hurdles you have to overcome in order to get the sailboat moving. One of the biggest is the frictional drag of the hull. You should be aware that every square foot of hull that is in contact with the water helps to slow the boat down. To reduce the amount of hull area that is in contact with the water, sailors sit on the leeward or low side and heel the boat to that side in light air as in Photo 14. Though a small amount of additional hull surface is immersed in the water on the lee side (mostly the topsides), much more of the underwater hull is lifted out on the windward side because of the rounded bottom. The net effect is a reduction of *wetted surface,* the amount of surface in contact with the water. The total result is reduced drag.

There's an added advantage to heeling the boat to leeward. The boom will stay on that side of the boat because of gravity rather than flop back and forth

Photo 14
*Heeling the boat when beating in light airs to
reduce wetted surface drag.*

which knocks the breeze out of the sails. Because the boom stays in one place, so does the mainsail. This allows the main to fall into the shape the sailmaker designed into it. Thus, when a zephyr of wind hits the sails, they are all ready to do their work. The airflow passes over the already curved sides of the sails and results in drive. Without this heeling, the initial breaths of air have to shape the sails first before effective sailing can start. Of course, when breaths of air are few and far between, your boat may never get up to a sustained movement through the water, unless the sails are properly shaped to begin with.

Windage is another large detrimental factor in light air sailing to windward. To cut this down, the skipper and crew should stay as low as possible on the deck or in the cockpit to avoid causing more wind resistance. Any mass attached to the boat that the air hits will slow down the boat's forward motion. Heavy thumping and jumping around the boat will also tend to slow it down.

The sails are operating at their greatest efficiency when the airflow is moving smoothly over the surface of the sail. And the same situation applies to water flow over the hull, keel and rudder. And because the keel and rudder are lifting surfaces, any reduction in their efficiency causes the boat to make more leeway and also be slower to windward. So this is why, in drifting conditions, the crew should walk as though they were on eggs, and they should sit quietly and make all their movements slowly and deliberately. On a boat with winches, you should use the winch handle to adjust the trim of a jib and do it by turning the winch click by click rather than manually pulling on the line. Any jerk of the jibsheet or mainsheet will disrupt the airflow over the sails.

In light air, a helmsman should hold the tiller very lightly in order to feel any slight tug put on the helm by the rudder. Though the helmsman should be sitting low in the boat, he or she must be able to see any dark patches on the water since this indicates a breeze. He or she must also develop the sensitivity to feel the direction of any slight breeze on the face.

Photo 15
Heeling the boat to weather helps speed on a run.

When you are running before the wind in light or drifting conditions you should again heel the boat. But this time you should do so to weather as in Photo 15. The crew in this photograph is not heavy, so the actual heel is rather slight. Nevertheless, note how the main boom is pointing up. What this does is lift the mainsail area higher off the surface of the water. Because every foot of increased altitude above the water surface means increased wind velocity, the mainsail now is in a stronger wind than it would be if it were not canted up at an angle. The increased velocity can be as much as 100 percent greater at heights of 35 feet than it is at two feet above the surface, though this does depend on wind strength.

Of course, this heeling to windward also reduces the wetted surface, just as heeling to leeward does. It also reduces weather helm, which is undesirable when you are running, by submerging more of the weather bow and by getting the center of effort of the sail plan more over the boat rather than having it out over the water where it can turn the boat to windward. And heeling to windward on a run also is good because it allows the spinnaker to fall, by gravity, out from behind the mainsail shadow and this exposes it to free air that is undisturbed by the main. Obviously this is a solid benefit.

When there's very little wind, *pumping* the sails can help get your boat moving downwind. To do this you grasp all the parts of the mainsheet, or grab the main boom itself, and pull as hard and fast as you can toward the center of the boat. Then let the main go slowly out again, and then quickly jerk it in again. These rhythmic fanning jerks, done every few seconds, will propel the boat forward.

Rolling the boat back and forth will also help move it forward. To do this, stand up and, holding onto the mast and shroud, throw your weight as violently as you can from one side to the other. The mainsheet should be trimmed in tightly. This maneuver will only be helpful if there's absolutely no wind and you are beginning to despair about getting anywhere. Of course your boat must also be quite small.

While the crew is rocking the boat in the manner I have described the helmsman can *scull* with the rudder. To do this, he or she pushes and pulls the tiller back and forth across the boat quite violently just as you would do with an oar. Surprisingly a pretty good turn of speed can be attained with this method. But don't try any of these rocking, pumping or sculling techniques while you are racing (unless the race committee says you may) or you'll be disqualified. All of these techniques are against the yacht racing rules unless otherwise stated by the race committee.

If you have tried all these things and you still aren't getting anywhere out on the water and you're about to miss dinner, the only thing I can suggest now is to break out the paddles or hail a friendly motorboat for a tow home. And next time you probably should think twice about getting so far away from home if it looks like a light air day.

HEAVY AIR SAILING

The words "heavy weather" always are subjective. The wind that is a "nice sailing breeze" for a San Francisco Sailor may be "heavy weather" for the sailor from Long Island. For our purposes, though, let's call heavy weather a wind that is blowing over 25 knots with lots of white caps and streaks of spume on the water.

Most beginning helmsmen are apt to get tense in heavy air, probably because it's much like riding a skittish horse: you never know when or where you're going to be thrown. Try to force yourself to relax.

Always hold onto the tiller or tiller extension with a firm, but not a tense grip. The latter is the "white knuckle" grip that often is used by less experienced sailors on windy days. If this tenseness is confined solely to your hand and forearm it's not a problem. However, the tense muscles do run right up into the upper arm and shoulder. This means that whenever the torso is moved, the tiller is as well.

On one of our school boats an instructor couldn't budge the tiller because the student's grip was so tight. Finally he had to move the entire body of the student to avoid a collision. But it is an example of how the rigidity can be transferred. Always try to think that your steering arm is an independent part of your body. Grip the boat all you want with your other arm, but consciously relax your steering arm.

While you are beating on any sized boat, you should sit to windward in heavy air. It's common, on some keelboats, to see helmsmen sitting down in the cockpit to leeward in heavy air. The trouble is that he can't see the approaching waves from that position.

If the waves are running in the same direction as the wind (about 40-45 degrees off your bow), the best way to play them is to head up, perhaps even pinch slightly, on the front side of the wave, then head off down the backside of the wave. This means you sail a short distance up the front of the wave when the wave's *current* or *orbital flow,* is against you, and you traverse along the backside where the *current* is with you. This reverse flow on the backside of the wave will help push you to windward.

With steep, short waves like the ones you can sometimes find in a current when it flows against a strong wind, heading off the wind at the crest of a wave also helps avoid the bone-jarring pounding that results from the boat literally falling into the next trough. Instead, it slides down the back of the retreating wave.

Unless a helmsman sits to windward, he is unable to see, and play, the waves, and this is a crucial part of heavy weather sailing. And he will not be able to see the ripples of a gust on the water as it approaches. When a 35-40 knot puff hits, the force is substantial and, since the apparent wind comes aft, it will have even more effect on the helmsman who hasn't headed up to meet it.

Tacking can be very difficult in heavy winds. The main problem is the wind resistance of the rigging, the flapping sails, and the resistance of the hull to the seas. If the boat isn't traveling fast to begin with, a skipper attempting to tack may end up in irons, head to wind and dead in the water. The wind and seas will quickly stop the boat, making the rudder useless. To avoid this, be sure you have adequate speed. Wait for a relatively calm spot (both wind and sea, if possible) before you attempt to tack. Tack at the crest of the wave when much of the bow and stern is out of the water. Less hull in the water means easier pivoting. It's very much like a skier making his turn on a mogul or mound of snow, when the ends of the skis are in the air.

The boat in Photo 16 has just fallen off the crest of a wave as you can see by the splash to leeward. To tack at this point will put the bow right into the next wave coming along. The boat in Photo 17 is just about to go up, and over, a wave. If he wants to tack, now is the best time to do it. When conditions are very rough and you have to be sure of completing the tack because of some obstruction, have your crew delay releasing the jibsheet. Let the jib back momentarily when

Photo 16
Don't tack while in the trough of a wave.

Photo 17
Tack at the crest of a wave.

you tack, but do so just long enough for the wind to help push the bow over to the new tack.

Running downwind in heavy weather can be wildly exciting and more than a little tense for any new helmsman. In such a situation it helps to rationalize and think ahead. Think about the worst that can happen, then say to yourself that even the worst isn't so terrible, so why worry about little things like being out of control, jibing wildly, broaching, etc. If you've ever had the "worst" happen, as I have, you'll know that it's all pretty quiet after you have lost a mast or you capsize. It's the wild speed and commotion short of the worst, that scares you. If you think about it in those terms, you'll perhaps find yourself even enjoying being at the very edge of control.

One major problem for the novice helmsman (and even for some who are experienced) when running in heavy winds and seas, is oversteering. The seas toss the boat around, threatening to jibe it one way, and broach it the other. An

Photo 18
Soling #620 is heading off to catch a wave . . .

Photo 19
*. . . and it pays off with a high speed surf that
leaves the others behind.*

already tense helmsman tends to overcorrect. By this I mean he or she still is steering in one direction when the boat already has changed its course to the same direction. For example, a boat may be swinging to starboard and the helmsman will steer to port to counteract the swing. But the boat then starts swinging to port before the helmsman has a chance to reverse the helm. The helmsman is trailing the boat's gyrations and actually reinforcing them.

The solution to this problem takes a strong will in the beginning, but it will become more natural and instinctive with some experience. The way to beat this is to try not to steer. Yes, I mean don't move the tiller more than a few inches either way. Probably at first you will steer horribly. But soon you will find that with proper anticipation and a good, hefty shove at just the proper time, very little rudder action is really needed. The boat won't sail in a perfect straight line, but in heavy seas you can't expect it to. You are, however, going to be sailing a much straighter course than one where you are using a lot of rudder.

Another requirement for a good heavy-weather downwind helmsman is surfing know-how. If the wind is so heavy that it precludes "pumping" (rapid trimming of the sails) the only way a boat can get up and stay on a surf is by good helmsmanship. To do this takes practice. But as a large wave approaches from astern, you should head up toward a reach to pick up speed — just like a surfboarder paddles furiously in front of a wave. When the stern starts to lift, head down the wave as boat #620 has done in Photo 18. Note in Photo 19 how US620 has left US622 far behind because of the good surfing ability of the helmsman. The bow wave is twice as high and the white wake indicates how fast it is moving. The trick is to aim your bow for the lowest part of the trough in the waves ahead. If it looks like you are going to overtake the wave ahead, start traversing the wave. When you lose the wave, keep an eye out astern for the next good one. When you see it coming, first head up for speed, then head off and start riding it.

Heavy weather helmsmanship takes practice, just like everything else. But if you shy away from sailing on heavy days, you'll never know how to handle such winds when you're caught out in them inadvertently. You'll never know whether your boat and crew can take it, and you'll never know how you will tackle the unusual problems that arise. You'll soon find that heavy weather sailing gives you a nice feeling of accomplishment when you come ashore at the end of the day.

WINGING THE JIB

Before we get into spinnaker work, there are times when we find it safer and less work to just wing out the jib with the spinnaker pole, particularly in heavy winds. Let's assume you are on starboard tack. Release both jibsheets. Grab the starboard jib sheet forward of the jib lead block with your right hand and snap the pole jaw over it with your left. Push the pole forward to the clew of the jib. Slide the pole straight forward just to windward of the jibstay. The pole should slide over your right hand with the jibsheet pressed against the underside of the pole and parallel to the pole. Don't try to push the pole to windward, just forward. When you have reached the inboard end of the pole, still holding the pole and jibsheet at the same time with your right hand, reach up and snap the inboard jaw into the ring of the mast. That done, keep tension on the jibsheet with your right hand and grab the sheet aft of the jib lead block with your left, taking in the slack. Then release the sheet with your right and trim normally. On port tack do everything with the opposite hand.

To properly trim a winged-out jib, pull the pole back as far as possible without letting the leech of the jib collapse or fold over. The leech of the jib should act like the luff. When it "luffs" let the pole forward. A topping lift and foreguy are not necessary because the clew of the jib will hold the pole up as long as the jibsheet is tight. The pole should be level or pointing downward. The higher the ring on the mast, the more the pole points down and the more pressure there is on the leech of the jib. In other words, if the top part of the leech is twisting off, raise the eye on the mast to correct it.

TEST QUESTIONS ON CHAPTERS I AND II

1. Is a sail with a free leech fuller or flatter than one with a tight leech?
2. What controls twist in a jib?
3. Are flat sails for speed or for power?
4. What are the threads called that run lengthwise in sailcloth?
5. What does the cunningham do?
6. Does heeling to windward decrease weather helm?
7. What is "roll tacking?"
8. Should you tack at the crest or the trough of a wave in heavy air?
9. What is "wetted surface?"
10. What is "pumping" a sail?

ANSWERS

1. Flatter.
2. Jib sheet tension. Fore and aft jib lead placement. Jib halyard.
3. Speed.
4. Warp.
5. Tensions the luff of a sail and keeps the draft from moving aft in heavy airs.
6. Yes.
7. Swinging the sails up towards the wind when tacking in light air by use of crew weight in order to keep the sails full.
8. The crest.
9. The amount of hull surface in contact with the water.
10. Rhythmically trimming a sail hard and easing it slowly to "fan" the boat forward.

CHAPTER III

SPINNAKER WORK

If you took Offshore Sailing School's Learn to Sail course you learned how to prepare a spinnaker for setting and how to set and douse it. You also learned basic trimming procedures. These will be reviewed as we practice with the spinnaker and you can reread *Colgate's Basic Sailing* on this subject. Here we want to delve deeper into spinnaker work.

COMMON SPINNAKER MISTAKES AND PROBLEMS

There is only one sure way to avoid problems with the spinnaker—don't set one. But if you don't, you'll also lose almost all of the pleasures of sailing a boat on a run. There are certain procedures to avoid or at least reduce the problems and others which will solve them faster.

For instance, the crew in Photo 20 will be able to get their spinnaker "sea anchor" aboard far easier if the skipper turns the boat right into the wind. The boat will stop and the water pressure filling the spinnaker disappears. Or, if they can't get the boat to turn into the wind, they should pull on just one corner of the spinnaker, so it can be brought aboard without water resistance. The following are some other common problems — and the easiest way to solve them:

Photo 21 shows what happens if the halyard is not clear all the way up before hoisting. When the topping lift was attached to the spinnaker pole, the halyard was between the pole and the topping lift. Either lower the halyard and untangle it, or disconnect the topping lift from the pole, let it go, and grab it again after the spinnaker has filled. Always make a last-second check before hoisting to make sure that the halyard is clear all the way up.

Wraps

This problem plays no favorites. Even large cruising boats with crackerjack crews can get spinnaker wraps. They happen when the spinnaker collapses for one reason or another and starts to rotate around itself. They can also occur as the spinnaker is hoisted if the corners of the spinnaker are not pulled apart quickly enough or if the bag has been inadvertently rotated before the set. When the wrap is very low in the spinnaker, it probably has to be lowered and sorted out. Never pull the pole back or head the boat up in order to fill the spinnaker on the assumption that the wrap will unwind if the spinnaker is full. It doesn't work and, in fact, makes the wrap tighter. Get the spinnaker in the dead air behind the main and jib and "blanket" it. Then shake it or pull down on the leech. The wrap shown in Photo 22 should come out with this method. If the wrap is high in the sail, releasing the halyard a few feet would allow the swivel, which may be jammed in the block, to rotate and unwind the spinnaker.

A bad type of wrap is one which winds around the jibstay. If it gets tight, it can be next to impossible to unwrap without cutting the spinnaker away. The problem is that a wire jibstay has strands that are twisted around each other. As

Photo 20
*A sea anchor is dragged astern to slow the boat down
during gales. It's usually a canvas bag (like a windsock)
not a spinnaker, as above.*

Photo 21
Spinnaker halyard caught under the topping lift.

the spinnaker is pulled down (assuming a crew member can reach the foot of the sail), it is rotated by the strands and gets tighter and tighter. Once a jibstay wrap occurs, jibe the main boom so the airflow off the mainsail is in the opposite direction. Instead of wrapping tighter, the spinnaker starts rotating in the opposite direction and unwrapping itself. I've known of this method for many years but never had to resort to it. Recently, however, one of our teaching boats developed a tight spinnaker wrap around the jib while running in a 25-knot wind. Nothing seemed to work, so we suggested (from a chase boat) that the crew jibe the mainsail. Within minutes this "impossible" wrap had completely unwound itself.

The type of wrap shown in Photo 23, which is low in the spinnaker and includes some extraneous lines for good measure, probably is incurable without lowering the spinnaker and starting anew.

Photo 22
A typical spinnaker wrap.

Photo 23
A very difficult wrap to solve.

Losing the Guy and Sheet

Often both the guy and sheet get free inadvertently. It sometimes happens during a jibe when one person is holding on to both and the spinnaker suddenly fills with a gust of wind. More often, it happens on the douse. The guy is released before someone has a hold on the sheet behind the mainsail on the leeward side. The sail goes flying out, as in Photo 24. One solution is to turn the boat dead downwind. In all but the heaviest winds, the spinnaker will come down within reach and can be gathered in. Another solution is to pull on just one line, either the guy or the sheet, and let the other trail free. As the corner gets close, ease the halyard. Premature halyard ease, however, runs the risk of having the spinnaker fill with air way out beyond the boat. When this happens the problem becomes serious. The boat may be pulled over so far that she fills with water and the heeling makes it impossible to turn the boat "into" the spinnaker (i.e. downwind) to relieve the pressure. Freeing the halyard completely, or cutting it, may become necessary. An obvious solution to the problem, stop knots in the end of the spinnaker, guy and sheet, is an absolute NO-NO! Far worse problems can result from such knots.

Premature Filling

Another common problem is having the spinnaker fill with wind before it is all the way up. On a small boat this can cause a capsize, and on a larger boat, such as a Soling, it may be difficult to raise the rest of the way because of the strain on the halyard. If the spinnaker fills prematurely, head directly downwind to blanket it behind the mainsail.

Losing the Halyard

Premature ease of the halyard before another crew member is prepared to gather it in, or inadequate securing (cleating) of the halyard after the spinnaker is

Photo 24
Someone released the guy and sheet prematurely.

raised, can cause the problem shown in Photo 25. If this halyard isn't caught and brought back up immediately, the spinnaker will either fill with water or be run through by the bow of the boat. Easing the halyard on the douse faster than it can be gathered in leads to the problems experienced by the crew in Photo 26. The head of the chute is about to fill with water, the weight of which will inevitably wrench the rest of the spinnaker from the grip of the crew. All this could have been avoided if the person easing the halyard had watched the person gathering and had tried not to get ahead of him or her.

SPINNAKER TRIM

There is no mystery about what makes a crew member a good spinnaker trimmer. It's experience and concentration, and neither of these can be taught. One is developed and the other innate. We can teach the basic rules of spinnaker trimming, but it depends on the person to eventually become good at it.

Photo 25
Halyard slipping can cause major problems.

Photo 26
The crew on the halyard eased faster than the spinnaker could be gathered in.

However, even the basic rules can be misleading. Nothing is hard and fast in sailing, and for every rule there's an exception or two. First, let's examine the general principles behind spinnaker trimming. When running, there's a little flow around the backside of the luff (from a crew member's vantage point), but that doesn't result in much drive. Therefore, we want the greatest projected area possible. Projected area is the area on a flat plane that is presented to the wind.

Just as a large parachute will let a man down more slowly than a small one, the more area of spinnaker exposed to the wind, the greater its effectiveness. This is done by keeping the pole well squared (aft) and the sheet well trimmed. The dotted line in Figure 22 shows the amount of area exposed to the wind with the pole forward. The dotted line in Figure 23 is much longer with the pole aft, indicating a greater "projected area."

If there weren't a price to pay for having the pole well aft, that's where we'd set it, but there is. As we square the pole aft, and also trim the sheet to keep the

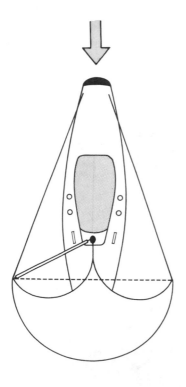 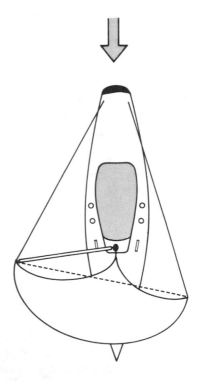

Figure 22
Pole forward: Spinnaker away from bad air of mainsail, but projected area small.

Figure 23
Pole aft: Projected area large, but spinnaker pulled into bad air from the mainsail.

spinnaker from collapsing, it is drawn in closer and closer to the mainsail. This means that the spinnaker is in the bad air of the main and loses efficiency. So we ease the pole forward and ease the sheet to get the chute away from the sail plan. Somewhere there is a happy medium between starving the spinnaker behind the main and losing projected area through too much ease, and this is where experience comes in.

The next general aspect of spinnaker trimming to remember is that a spinnaker is a symmetrical sail and should look symmetrical when flown. Although there are a few exceptions to this, such as when close reaching or in light air, it is generally true. If the spinnaker is misshapen, as in Photo 27, because the pole is too high or too low, it will lose much of its effectiveness. Keeping the above two general aspects of spinnaker trimming in mind, all the rest of the basic rules fall in place.

Following are some of the requirements for pole position. A good starting point is to set the pole square to the apparent wind. The masthead fly is in undisturbed air and is a good guide. Set the pole at right angles to it. As the boat sails further downwind, however, air over the main tends to flow forward and around the mast, making the spinnaker practically by the lee. This means that the pole will need to be squared back, past perpendicular to the masthead fly. Actually, it will be perpendicular to the shroud telltales. I would use the masthead fly until the wind is well aft and then switch to shroud telltales.

There are some unusual cases where the masthead fly isn't very accurate for spinnaker trimming, such as on a 12-Meter yacht. Being a ¾ rig, the head of the spinnaker is considerably lower than the masthead fly and the apparent wind at the top of the mast is noticeably farther aft than that at pole height, due to increased wind velocity aloft. Another exception to setting the pole perpendicular to the apparent wind is when you are using a very short foot spinnaker. In that case, squaring the pole brings the clew near the jibstay and much of the projected area is lost.

Photo 27
*A distorted spinnaker can be caused by improper pole height
and reduce efficiency.*

The pole should generally be level — not parallel to the water as I continually hear people saying, but perpendicular to the mast. This means that if you raise or lower the outboard end of the pole, you should raise or lower the inboard end (the end attached to the mast) a corresponding amount. The idea is to get the spinnaker as far away from the sail plan as possible, but to insist on keeping the pole level to achieve this is overkill. A pole has to be cocked 25° from the level to decrease its effective length 10% and during the first 20° only 5% is lost, so a few degrees off of level really doesn't make much difference. Probably more is lost by fussing around with inboard pole height than is gained by having the pole exactly level. Also, a slight cock upward will put the pole in line with the guy and reduce the bending strain on the pole.

More important is the height at which the whole pole is set. The general rule is to keep the tack and clew of the spinnaker level with the plane of the deck (not with the water). But this really goes back to keeping the spinnaker symmetrical.

Photo 28
Fairly tight slot betweeen luffs of jib and spinnaker.

Photo 29
Raising the pole opens the slot.

When the two corners are level, the spinnaker is symmetrical, looks good, and flies well.

The exceptions to this occur mainly while reaching, and in either high or low wind velocities. While reaching, particularly when flying the spinnaker with the jib set, the tack of a normal reaching spinnaker on a class boat can be set higher than the clew. This opens the slot between the spinnaker and the jib. It also eases the luff of the spinnaker and flattens the chute. Photo 28 shows the tack and clew fairly even. There is little space between the jib and spinnaker luffs. The pole on the center boat in Photo 29 is quite high and the slot is open, but the spinnaker is misshapen. The boat on the right in the same photo has the best spinnaker set of all. With a flat, tight reaching spinnaker, the reverse is true. The tack (the pole end) should be set quite low and the luff set like a genoa on a pole.

Once the pole is set correctly, it's fairly simple to play the spinnaker. The sheet should be eased until one sees a slight curl along the luff as in Photo 30, and then trimmed to make the curl disappear. This must be done constantly and is

Photo 30

Ease the sheet until a curl appears along the luff, then trim.

Photo 31

This spinnaker is "starved" for air. The sheet should be eased, the pole squared, or both.

where concentration plays its biggest part. Quite often the novice overtrims the spinnaker, which gets in the disturbed air behind the mainsail and collapses as in Photo 31. This is called a "starve." Pull the pole aft to correct the problem.

The spinnaker guy should also be played if you are running in a slop. As the boat rolls to windward, the pole must be squared and the sheet eased. As it rolls to leeward, the pole should be eased forward and the sheet trimmed.

All changes in apparent wind direction necessitate changes in pole position and sheet trim. If the boat starts surfing, if it falls off a plane, or if the wind velocity changes, the apparent wind direction will be affected and the spinnaker trimmer will have to make adjustments. Moreoever, he must learn to anticipate these changes ahead of time.

HALYARD EASE

There are times when one should ease the spinnaker halyard, but when is it good to ease it off — and how much?

The next time you are on a reach with the spinnaker set, look up behind the mainsail on the lee side. Then ease the spinnaker halyard six inches or so while looking at the leech of the sail, not the head. It will become obvious how much the slot between the spinnaker and the main will open up to allow free air passage.

When running downwind in a breeze, easing the halyard has two effects. First, it gets the spinnaker away from the disturbed air of the mainsail, and second, it allows the spinnaker to be more vertical than it is when fully hoisted. In light air, however, the halyard shouldn't be eased, since the spinnaker will just come straight down. Nor should it be eased on a reach in heavy air, because the sail's center of effort will go out further over the water and possibly cause a broach. On a run in heavy air, an eased spinnaker will be more apt to roll from one side of the boat to the other (oscillate) than one fully hoisted. In short, easing the halyard is rarely done on a run and is really only beneficial on a medium air reach.

SPINNAKER BROACHING

No matter what size sailboat you sail, if you set a spinnaker in heavy air, you will probably broach at one time or another. Fifteen-footers broach and 80-footers broach. Size is no deterrent.

A mild form of broaching is shown in Photo 32. It is essentially an overpowering weather helm caused by a number of factors. When the weather helm (the tendency for the boat to round up into the wind) becomes so strong that the helmsman is unable to counteract it with the rudder, the boat will broach. Most of the time this means that the boat will just wallow broadside to the wind until steering control is regained and the boat can be headed back downwind.

A major factor causing broaching is heeling. As mentioned before, excessive heeling causes a tremendous weather helm as the bow wave pushes the hull to weather. The helmsman has to steer the boat well to leeward to keep her sailing straight.

Contributing to additional weather helm is the fact that the force in the sails is out over the water when heeled. Let's fantasize for a moment. Imagine that in Photo 32 we have tied a line around the mast just above the spreaders and have run it all the way to shore where we've tied it to the back of a car. Now, we drive the car inland pulling the mast faster than the hull of the boat can keep up. By looking at the photo and using your imagination, it should be clear that first the boat will rotate until it is parallel to the shore, and then the car will be dragging the whole mess shoreward by the mast. The hull at this point will be dragging sideways through the water, creating such resistance that the mast will be almost lying in the water from the pull of the line.

With the spinnaker out over the water, the total wind force affects the boat in exactly the same way as our imaginary line to the shore. The more the boat rotates into the wind, the more it heels, until we have a full-fledged broach on our hands.

In a broach, the rudder becomes next to worthless. The boat is lying on its side, so the rudder is near the surface where it can't get a "bite." Since the rudder is more parallel to the surface than vertical and perpendicular to the surface, steering to leeward has much the same effect as the elevators on the tail of an airplane. The stern and keel will lift rather than turn. So the more the boat heels, the less effective the rudder becomes in turning it back downwind to reduce the heel. In fact, the rudder will start to increase the heel after a certain amount of heel is reached.

If, in the early stages of a broach, the helmsman is able to turn the boat so that the hull is parallel to the direction of pull (on our imaginary line to the shore), the hull has less resistance and a better chance of keeping up with the sails. In

Photo 32
A broach.

other words the helmsman should try to steer the hull of the boat under the rig, keeping the mast as vertical as possible. The tendency to broach will be reduced. To facilitate catching the broach before it develops, the skipper and crew can take certain precautions.

Since heeling is the enemy, they must hike out hard during gusts of wind that could precipitate a broach. The crew in Photo 32 have not done this and are about to pay for it. Another way to reduce heeling is to luff the sails. Since the spinnaker gives the boat a great deal of drive, it is the last sail to luff. First, luff the mainsail. Remember — if your boom vang is on tight, the boom is being held down. As the main is luffed, the boom end goes into the water and is pushed back toward the center of the boat. This is shown clearly in Photo 32. Since the main can't be eased, more heeling will occur and the boom will be pushed even closer to the hull by the water flow. This will cause even more heeling and another vicious cycle starts, until a broach occurs. So, ease the boom vang. In fact, many racers disregard the mainsheet and play only the boom vang to avoid a broach. The boom lifts as the vang is eased and the top part of the sail, near the head, luffs first. Since this is the part that causes most of the heeling, the sailor is reducing heeling without detracting much from the general drive of the sail.

The next sail to ease is the jib, if one is being used under the spinnaker. It is fallacious to think that trimming the jib will reduce weather helm by blowing the bow to leeward. Whatever lee helm could develop by this method is nullified by the weather helm caused by the additional heeling of the jib when trimmed tightly.

When it is obvious that drastic measures are needed to avoid a broach, the spinnaker can be collapsed by easing the sheet a couple of feet. The helmsman must anticipate the need for this and give the command to the spinnaker trimmer to "break" the spinnaker. When the boat has been steered back downwind and has straightened up, the spinnaker can be trimmed again to fill it.

There are a few other factors that can contribute to broaching. If the spinnaker halyard has stretched or is not all the way up, the center of effort of the spinnaker (its "pull") will be further out over the water and aggravate the turning moment. The tack of the spinnaker should be right at the end of the spinnaker pole for the same reason. If the pole is too high, as in Photo 32, the luff will have a large curve to leeward, causing the drive to be further out over the water. And if the leech of the spinnaker is cupped, as in the photo, rather than flat and free, the trapped air will cause more heeling.

Crew weight should be aft on reaches for two reasons. First, the forward force on the sails against the resistance of the hull will have a natural tendency to bury the bow and lift the stern. This tendency is pronounced in many catamaran designs when reaching. They tend to bury the bow of the lee hull and actually "trip" over it (capsize). The crew has to move way back near the stern of the weather hull. Second, crew weight aft keeps the rudder deeper in the water and increases its effectiveness.

ROLLING OR OSCILLATING

Photo 33 shows another problem in spinnaker work: rolling, or oscillating. The boat in the photo is rolling by the lee and will shortly roll in the opposite direction. In heavy seas this can become wildly exciting. Your boat is almost jibing as the mast rolls to windward, nearly broaching as it heels to leeward. Most of the problem is caused by allowing the spinnaker too much freedom.

In the photo, the sheet has been eased beyond the jibstay (hidden from view) so the spinnaker is able to get completely around to the starboard side of the boat. It then pulls the mast over in that direction. As it heels, the starboard bow wave develops and shoves the bow to port, toward a jibe. The helmsman steers the boat hard in the opposite direction, the spinnaker oscillates over to the port side of the boat, causing heeling and a strong weather helm which, again, the helmsman counteracts. Thus the rolling starts. If there is any ease in the halyard,

Photo 33
Rolling.

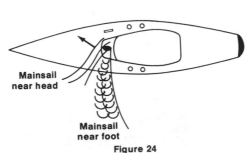

Mainsail near head

Mainsail near foot

Figure 24
Twist causes the upper part of the sail to pick up air flow and aggravates rolling.

the spinnaker is free to spin in a large arc. Pulling the halyard up very tightly reduces the rolling.

Off the wind in heavy air, the mainsail becomes a large factor in control, particularly on small boats. A powerful boom vang is a must. If the boom is allowed to lift in the air, the top of the leech will fall off so far that it may actually point forward of abeam, or at least be folding over the spreader and shrouds. Figure 24 is a cross section of the sail near the foot and another cross section near the head. Note that while the foot of the sail is stalled, the top part of the sail is getting airflow over the lee side, creating lift in the direction of the arrow. This tends to pull the top of the mast to windward, making the boat roll to windward. Once started, each subsequent roll is a little more severe. The apparent wind goes more forward and flow is picked up lower down in the sail each time the mast rolls to weather, and the faster it rolls, the more forward the apparent wind goes. The more forward the apparent wind goes, the greater the area of mainsail that develops airflow on the lee side, and the greater the lift. The greater the lift, the faster the mast swings to windward, and so on, until the boat is rolling madly. The solution is to vang down strongly and, if the vang can't handle the forces, to trim the mainsheet in a little so the top part of the sail is also stalled. Though the vang in Photo 33 appears to be fairly tight, we can see by the shadows in the mainsail that the top part is well forward of the bottom, so more vang tension would be helpful.

When rolling conditions exist, consider trimming the jib in flat. It will help to keep the bow downwind, and helps dampen the rolling like a baffle. Changing course to more of a reach can also help. Further, in such conditions we want to reduce the effectiveness of the spinnaker. By easing the pole forward of square with the apparent wind and by overtrimming the sheet, we can roll part of the spinnaker in behind the mainsail, thereby partially blanketing it. This also keeps the spinnaker from picking up airflow on the lee side, which, like the main, pulls the spinnaker over to the weather side of the boat and rolls the mast to wind-

Photo 34
A spinnaker flying out beyond the pole.

ward. Lower the pole to keep the spinnaker in closer to the sail plan of the boat, but don't overdo it. Lowering the pole excessively on a running chute makes the luff fuller in cross section and more likely to collapse. In heavy winds the jolt of the spinnaker filling after having been collapsed can easily break something. Make sure the pole foreguy is tight so the pole can't swing back as the boat heels to windward. Never let the tack of the spinnaker fly out beyond the pole end, as in Photo 34. It can cause wild rolling.

Place your crew weight on opposite sides of the boat. Just as children can seesaw faster if they're closer to the middle of the seesaw than when sitting at the very ends, the boat will roll less if the crew weight is spread out wide apart. And, last, change helmsmen if it appears that the present one doesn't quite have the anticipation or timing to counteract the rolling.

As with all sailing, don't accept problems such as broaching and rolling as unavoidable. Certainly, they can happen to any crew, but one should work at reducing the problem to more acceptable and manageable terms.

LIGHT AIR SPINNAKER WORK

Spinnaker trimming in light air takes a great deal of patience. Lower the pole way down, but always keep the pole end a little higher than the clew. Then, when a puff of air comes and fills the spinnaker, the pole will be at the proper height. In other words, keep the pole at the proper height for the 10% of the time that the spinnaker is filled and doing the boat some good, not the 90% of the time when it is drooping and not producing any forward drive. Another reason to keep the pole a little higher than the clew in light air is that a low pole will stretch the luff and fold it over (see Photo 35). When a puff arrives, the spinnaker is unable to fill because of the shape of the luff.

Photo 35
An excessively low pole tightens the luff and causes the spinnaker to collapse more easily.

The same thing can happen with some very full-shouldered running spinnakers. The luff can collapse from a starve and though you know you must pull the pole aft, first you have to overtrim the sheet to unfold the luff. Only then can you pull the pole back with the spinnaker full. It is better in light air to have the pole too low rather than too high, as this causes the spinnaker to droop to leeward and it will need a much stronger puff to fill it.

Another light air problem is caused by the jib. Air flowing past the lee side of the jib causes a suction on a reach, and if the spinnaker collapses, it sucks into the jib and is very difficult to fill it again. The natural tendency is to trim the jib to get it away from the spinnaker, but actually the opposite should be done. The first time the spinnaker collapses, free the jib sheet to break down the airflow over the jib. If it happens a few more times, take the jib down.

JIBING THE SPINNAKER

End for End

Spinnaker jibes seem to be a great bugaboo for most crews. Though almost any crew can get into trouble, sometimes it is very difficult to analyze the problem. A jibe happens fast and all crew members have tasks to perform. When you're busy with your own job, it is often hard to notice where things are going wrong. Most of the time the person on the foredeck who is all wrapped up in spinnaker cloth, lines, etc., is the butt of abuse when actually the fault lies with the person steering.

The skipper who turns the boat too sharply and gives the crew inadequate time or directions will almost certainly cause a bad jibe. In heavy air, the helmsman must be sure to counteract the tendency for the boat to round up into the wind right after a jibe. The boom swings over with a great deal of force and, when it reaches the end of the mainsheet, it stops abruptly and the sail creates a wall to the wind. Something has to give until an equilibrium is found, so the boat heels over and a strong weather helm results. The forces in the sail out over the water turn the bow of the boat toward the wind. This combination of factors will cause a broach in heavy winds unless the helmsman heads the boat off decisively to meet the anticipated turning moment. Done properly, the boat, though being steered as if to jibe back again, just sails straight ahead. Nothing can make a crew look worse than a bad helmsman.

But, to be fair about this, some of the worst problems are caused by the crew handling the spinnaker guy and sheet. A "reach-to-reach" jibe is one in which the boat is turned from a reach with the pole on or near the jibstay on one tack to a reach with the pole near the jibstay on the opposite tack. It is a difficult type of jibe because the boat is turned so far, approximately 90°. The spinnaker has to get completely around to the other side, and problems occur if this is not done with alacrity.

Photos 36, 37, 38 portray the problem. As the boat heads down from the starboard tack reach in order to jibe, the pole should come aft and the sheet

Photo 36
Preparing for a reach to reach jibe. Sheet should be more eased.

Photo 37
At the point of jibing, pole should be pulled aft.
Here it's still forward.

Photo 38
After jibing to port tack, spinnaker should be on the starboard side
of the boat. Here it's still on the port side.

should be eased. After all, the boat is on a dead run at the instant of jibing and the spinnaker should be trimmed properly for that point of sailing. The jibe of the main boom and spinnaker pole is then completed and the boat heads up to the new port tack reach. The pole should be on the jibstay and the sheet trimmed in. In photo 37, nothing of the sort has happened. At the point of jibing, the spinnaker is still on the port side of the boat, the same side as the wind is about to come over. After the jibe, the spinnaker starts to blow through between the jib and the main as in Photo 39. When this happens, about the only solution is to head back downwind to blow the spinnaker forward around the jibstay.

During the jibe, the foredeck crew on a boat like a Soling should stand, back against the mast, facing forward, as in Photo 40. From this position, he has much more leverage for controlling the pole and getting it off the mast. Also, he can see the spinnaker and help keep it full. On a reach-to-reach jibe, he should take the pole off the mast and then off the old guy. This makes the spinnaker free-wheeling and the mid-cockpit crew can pull the spinnaker around the boat

Photo 39

The spinnaker, now on the windward side of the boat after the jibe, blows through between the jibstay and the mast.

Photo 40

During a jibe, foredeck crew faces forward with back braced against mast.

without the pole restricting it in any way. The foredeck crew then connects the end of the pole that was previously on the mast to the new guy and snaps the other end of the pole onto the mast fitting. This is called "end for ending" the pole.

When the pole is not taken completely off the spinnaker, the foredeck crew has to be extremely quick not to end up in the situation shown in Photo 41. The crew here decided to snap the end that came off the mast on to the new guy before snapping it from the old guy. The cockpit crew has pulled the spinnaker around to the starboard side, but cannot pull it any further because the pole is against the shrouds. The jibe has been completed and the spinnaker is starting to blow in between the jib and the main. If the pole were not attached, the spinnaker could have been pulled all the way around to the starboard side even if the foredeck crew was having trouble getting organized.

A running jibe is much easier. The boat's heading changes only slightly, so all we are basically doing is changing the pole from one side to the other while keeping the spinnaker full. Photo 42 shows a running jibe at midstage. The foredeck crew is in a good position, back braced against the mast and feet spread apart for balance. In light winds as shown, the skipper should hold the main boom in the middle of the boat for a short time to keep the spinnaker full while the pole is being transferred to the other side. In the case of a running jibe, the pole may be left attached to the old guy until the other end is snapped over the new guy. Thus, the foredeck crew can help keep the spinnaker full during the jibe. Photo 43 is taken at the point when the jibe is almost completed. The foredeck crew should have the pole on the new guy and should be attaching the other end to the mast, so he is a little behind schedule (or the skipper is a little ahead, depending on your point of view).

Photo 41
Foredeck crew should have disconnected old guy
before jibing. Now pole is against starboard shrouds and
spinnaker cannot be pulled further around the jibstay.

Photo 42

A running jibe.

Photo 43

A running jibe almost completed.

Photo 44

Windward spinnaker douse: Get pole out of the way first.

Photo 45

Then gather the spinnaker in to windward pulling on the guy.

DOUSING THE SPINNAKER

Taking a spinnaker down to leeward is quite simple — the only major problem is caused by letting it get out from behind the mainsail into strong, unobstructed wind. The crew gathering in the chute must have control of the sail by bringing the sheet forward to a spot just behind the shrouds. The guy is then eased and the halyard lowered, as the sail is pulled in behind the mainsail. On small boats, if someone lets the guy go before the sheet is under control, the chute will go flying aft to the stern and will be the devil to gather in.

There may be times when a windward douse is in order. If you plan to set the spinnaker again and the next set is on the other tack, a windward take-down will prepare you properly for the next set. On windy days a windward take-down also avoids having to send a crew to leeward to grab the sheet.

Take the pole down before you intend to douse (Photo 44) and then just pull the spinnaker around to windward with the new guy as the halyard is lowered (Photo 45). Many smaller boats set and douse the spinnaker to windward as a matter of course.

TEST QUESTIONS ON CHAPTER III

1. What's the last thing to do before pulling the spinnaker up?
2. Should you head up to fill the sail when you have a wrap?
3. If the spinnaker collapses with a jib set, what should you do about the jib?
4. What does easing the spinnaker halyard do? When should it be eased?
5. To help avoid broaching, should crew weight be forward or aft?
6. If the spinnaker halyard is eased a little, will rolling be more aggravated or more controlled?
7. In light air should the spinnaker pole be lower or higher than the rest of the sail generally?
8. Should the foredeck crew face forward or aft when jibing the spinnaker?
9. If you are on port tack and the next set will be on starboard, should you take the spinnaker down to windward or to leeward?
10. What is "projected area?"

ANSWERS

1. Check that the halyard is clear right to the top.
2. No.
3. Ease it. If the spinnaker continues to collapse, douse the jib.
4. Opens the slot between the jib and spinnaker. On a medium air reach.
5. Aft.
6. More aggravated.
7. Higher.
8. Forward.
9. Windward.
10. The area of the spinnaker on a flat plane that is presented to the wind.

CHAPTER IV

NAVIGATION

Navigation is broken down into two categories — celestial navigation and piloting. The former is navigation based on the position of the celestial bodies and is normally used out of sight of land. Since the manual is for sailors in small boats, we will stick with piloting which is navigation by reference to landmarks, buoys, soundings and the like.

THE CHART

The chart is a neat "road map" of the sea printed by the U.S. Department of Commerce and available at many nautical supply stores. The area a chart covers and the identifying number is listed in a nautical chart catalog. Photo 46 shows a section of this catalog. If I'm sailing out of Port Washington, N.Y., for instance, I look at the catalog sheet, note that chart #12366 is needed (the circle in Photo 46).

For very small boats, the Small Craft Series of charts is handy because they are prefolded compactly and don't need a large, flat surface to spread on. Also, one chart, like #12363 in Photo 46, covers the same area that a number of the other charts cover, so it's more economical to purchase.

Photo 46

A portion of a catalog of charts.

59

As can be seen in the catalog, charts come in different scales. They are all roughly the same actual size, but cover different sized areas. Chart #12366, for instance, covers only a small portion of chart #12363, yet blows it up to the same size as #12363. Since #12366 enlarges a small area, it is called a "large-scale" chart. Such charts are used for entering harbors where precision and accuracy is more necessary than when in open water. If you're planning a trip, a smaller scale chart such as #12363 covers more distance and is easier to use.

The traditional equipment used are still the parallel rulers to move a course or bearing on the chart from the compass rose to your position or the landmark's, and dividers to measure distance. Though those two items are all one needs, others have been developed that some sailors find helpful to use, the protractor, for instance. The protractor is laid on the chart so one edge is parallel to a line of longitude. This gives it a reference to true north. The center of the plastic square is a compass rose so when the arm is rotated to the desired course, it gives you a true course line. Some such protractors have a double compass rose. The second one can be rotated to adjust for variation, so the arm will show a magnetic course.

DISTANCES

For the purpose of navigation the earth is considered spherical. The north pole is named for the top of the globe and the south pole is the bottom. Lines running north and south around the earth passing through these two imaginary poles are called meridians of longitude. The horizontal lines are parallels of latitude. Since a circle is 360°, the parallel lines of latitude divide the earth into 360 equal parts of 60 nautical miles each. There are 60 minutes to a degree, so one minute of latitude is equivalent to one nautical mile, which is somewhat longer than the statute mile we use ashore.

To measure the distance between points A and B in Photo 47 we use a pair of dividers. We place one tip on point A and the other on point B. Now, place the dividers along the edge of the chart, as in Photo 48 and count the number of minutes of latitude (shown as alternate dark and light increments, each divided into tenths) that fall between the two tips. In this case it's 3.15 minutes, which converts to 3.15 nautical miles. If we sail that distance in one half hour, we are sailing at 6.3 knots. A knot is one nautical mile sailed in one hour.

If the distance you want to measure is greater than the spread attainable by the dividers, spread them along the edge of the chart a workable number of miles (minutes of latitude), say five miles from tip to tip. Then lay one tip on your starting point. The other will rest on a spot five miles down the course. Walk the dividers so that the first tip lays five miles further down the course, and so on, until your destination is reached. It would be unusual for the last measurement to be exactly five miles, so the dividers will probably have to be pressed together so the tip rests on the destination, and this reduced distance can be measured on the edge of the chart.

To measure long distances on a 1:80,000 scale chart where only a rough estimation of distance is needed, I use my hand. The spread between my thumb and little finger is almost exactly 10 miles (Photo 49) and I can measure 70 or 80

Photo 47

A course line is drawn from Smith Rock (A) to Greens Ledge (B).

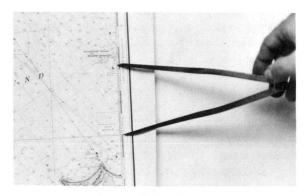

Photo 48

Place dividers along the edge of the chart to measure distance.

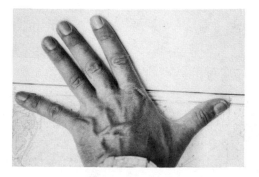

Photo 49

A hand spread on many charts is almost exactly ten miles.

mile distances quickly and within a few miles of accuracy. Check your hand spread. Perhaps you can use this method also.

READING A CHART

Look at the section of a chart shown in Photo 50. Buoys are shown as small diamonds with a dot or circle underneath to indicate their exact location. A purple color around the dot means it's a lighted buoy. The color of the diamond, usually red or green corresponds to the color of the buoy. To the right of center we see a black diamond. Next to it is the number "23" in quotes. Anything in quotes is written on the buoy. Even numbers are on red buoys and odd numbers are on green. The chart also indicates that the buoy is a bell.

The information on Execution Rocks lighthouse is given next to it. We interpret the information to mean that it flashes a white light every 10 seconds. The light is 62 feet above sea level and has a 22 mile visibility. It sounds a horn during foggy periods and also is a radio beacon with a frequency of 286 kilohertz.

The red and black diamond marked "RB" on the left in Photo 50 indicates a junction buoy, meaning you can pass on either side. Since the letter "N" (nun) follows the "RB," the actual buoy (which has red and black horizontal bands) will show a red band uppermost. This means that the preferred channel would be as if the buoy were all red. We leave red buoys to starboard as we enter a harbor or sail from a larger body of water to a smaller one. The simple phrase to remember this fact is "Red-Right-Returning."

There are many other items of information on the chart. Note the colors. White areas are deep, navigable water, light-blue areas are usually under 20 feet deep, and green areas are out of the water at low tide. The depths of the water are usually marked in feet at mean low water. Extreme low water could mean depths four or five feet less than shown on the chart, so take that into account. Along the East Coast of the U.S. the tides are semi-diurnal: two high tides and two low

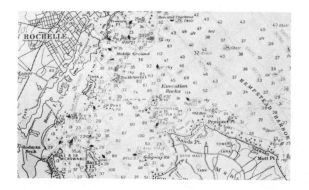

Photo 50

A section of a chart showing a wide variety of navigational aids.

tides in a 24-hour period. The tide height changes about 25% the first and last two hours of a tide, and about 50% during the middle two hours. This is a factor to take into consideration if it's necessary to cross a bar or a shoal that you know is too shallow for your boat at dead low tide, yet has deep enough water at certain times during the tidal fall. The U.S. Government prints the book Tide Tables, giving the predicted times of high and low water and the heights of the tide. On some charts the depths (soundings) may be in meters or fathoms (six feet equals one fathom), so check the explanation on the chart itself.

Also shown on charts are depth contours. These contour lines connect all the areas of equal depth and are very useful in navigation with the depth finder.

On the yellow part of the chart indicating dry land, any object which could be helpful in obtaining a navigational fix is located and marked. Tanks, towers, conspicuous buildings, spires, and others are all pinpointed.

VARIATION AND DEVIATION

Variation is described in Offshore Sailing School's Learn to Sail course. It is the angle between the geographic meridian (a line passing through the geographic poles—north and south) and the local magnetic meridian (a line passing through the magnetic poles). In other words, your compass will point to the magnetic north pole and at any given point this will be so many degrees to the west or east of true north which points to the geographic north pole. In a few spots on earth there is no variation and your magnetic compass will point to true north. Your chart will have the number of degrees of variation written on it for the given area.

Deviation was also described in the Learn to Sail course. It's the compass error caused by the metal on the boat that attracts the compass needle. On sailboats it rarely amounts to much but should be taken into account for accuracy even if it's only a degree. This error is measured when a compass adjuster "swings" your compass and, by the use of magnets, reduces the error caused by the magnetic pull of metal on the boat. It's the difference in direction the compass needle should point to, taking variation into account, and the direction it does point. The adjuster may not be able to correct all the deviation so will make a deviation table. This shows you the deviation for various boat headings.

You can determine your deviation in a less formal manner and correct it yourself. Place your boat next to a navigational aid with a known position such as a buoy. Draw a line on your chart north from the buoy (allowing for variation) and note which landmark in the distance the line passes through. Point your boat at the same landmark and see what your compass reads. The difference is deviation. By adjusting the magnets on the side of the compass, reduce the deviation by one-half. Then head east and determine the deviation in that direction. Reduce it by one-half by adjusting the magnets on the front and back of the compass. Continue with south, then west and then repeat the process all over again until most of the deviation is gone.

Both variation and deviation errors are expressed as either easterly errors (the compass needle points to the east of true north) or westerly errors (the needle points to the west of true north). They can be combined. For instance, if the variation is 10° E and the deviation is 2° W, the net compass error is 8° E. If variation is 8° W and deviation is 1° W, the net error is 9° W.

By combining the errors we can use a very simple acronym to determine direction: CADET, which stands for Compass, ADd East for True. In other words, if you have your compass heading, just add any easterly combined compass errors to obtain the true heading. By just remembering CADET, all the rest falls into place logically. If you add easterly errors, you subtract westerly errors. If you have your true course from the chart and you want to know what compass course to steer, you reverse the procedure and substract easterly errors and add westerly errors.

Let's say you have taken a bearing on a lighthouse to obtain your position. It bears 276°. Your deviation is 1° E and your variation is 7° E. Your chart does not have a magnetic compass rose on it, only a true one. You add 8° to 276° and find that the true bearing is 284° which you plot on the chart.

Once you've determined your position you set a new course for your boat, walk the parallel rulers over to the true compass rose and determine that your true course is 093°. What will be the course the helmsman will steer using your compass aboard? With a compass error of 8° E, we subtract it from 093° because we are going from true to compass, not compass to true as in the acronym, CADET. The answer is 085°.

DEAD RECKONING

Your "dead reckoning position" (DR) is the position determined by applying your course and distance from a previously determined position. There are a number of theories how it came to be called "dead" reckoning. One is that it's short for "deduced" reckoning because your position is being deducted from the input of your speed and distance. That "dead" was "ded" in middle English lends some credence to this theory. At the opposite end of the theory spectrum is that "dead" means "exact" as in a "dead shot" or "dead ahead." Dead reckoning, therefore, is as exact a reckoning of position as can be obtained with the variables existing.

A third and more intriguing possibility was that it came from the log used on early sailing ships called a chip log. It was made from a flat triangular chip of wood with lines from each corner that met a few feet away where they were attached to a single towline. The result was like a sea anchor that remained stationary when in the water. Along the towline were equally spaced knots and the line was coiled on a spindle much like that used to fly a kite. To measure the speed of the sailing ship, the chip log was put over the side and the line ran out. A 28 second sand glass was turned upside down and the number of knots that passed through the crewman's fingers by the time the sand ran out was equal to the number of nautical miles the ship was traveling per hour. So, though the knots originally were units of distance, they soon became known as units of speed with a built in sense of "per hour" which is why we never say "knots per hour." If five knots passed through his fingers, to say "five knots per hour" would be inaccurate because it was five knots in 28 seconds. "Dead reckoning" most likely came from reckoning your position to the point where your chip log was dead in the water since you didn't measure your speed all the time — only when you wanted to update your position (or if there was a significant change in wind strength).

PLOTTING

Since sailboats are subject to the vagaries of the wind it's very difficult to set a particular course and speed in order to end up at a desired destination on a given schedule. Of course you can set an initial course and determine your ETA (estimated time of arrival) based on the speed you are making through the water adjusted for current, which gives you your speed and course over the bottom. But if the wind dies you won't make the speed you based your calculations on and you'll spend longer in the current which will require a course adjustment. If the wind shifts, your speed may change because you're on a different point of sailing, either faster or slower, even if the wind velocity doesn't change. The wind may shift further so you no longer can lay the course you originally desired and have to beat for your destination. In short, you are constantly updating your position as you sail along and are forever changing the course to your destination. The navigator who doesn't keep careful track of his DR plot will get lost.

First we must start from a known position. We plot our course to the destination and after we have traveled awhile we plot the distance we have covered on the course we've been steering and mark it as our dead reckoning position with the time as in Figure 25. We use the 24-hour clock in navigation, so 1515 in the diagram is 3:15 p.m. Just add 12 hours to any p.m. time to get the 24 hour clock time. Always use four digits so 9:18 a.m. is marked as 0918. Courses

Figure 25

are written with three digits as 093 in the diagram. If it was written "93" a person reading another's writing might mistake a line or a smudge and read "193" or "293." We add "M" to the course to show it's magnetic or "T" for true. If you're using a chart with a magnetic compass rose and courses drawn on it are always magnetic, you may start deleting the "M."

An hour after your first DR you update your position and discover three good landmarks or navigational aids to take bearings from. In Figure 26 a radio tower marked on the chart bears 020°, a buoy bears 170° and a point of land has just obscured another point of land behind it. I use the third method all the time because you don't have to take a bearing and be subject to the possible errors caused by the compass swinging or by your parallel rulers slipping, etc. Each of these bearings is a line of position to the object. Where two or more LOP's cross you have a "Fix." You plot the bearings on the chart and get a small triangle. If you're lucky you may get all three lines to cross at exactly the same spot. Nevertheless, a small triangle is accurate enough a position to call it a "Fix." You mark the fix and the time, and plot a new course to your destination, in this case 094M. If you have a log that reads the number of miles you have been sailing it's always good to note the log reading on the chart at the time of the fix. Also, if you have a fathometer, check the depth of the water at the time of the fix and

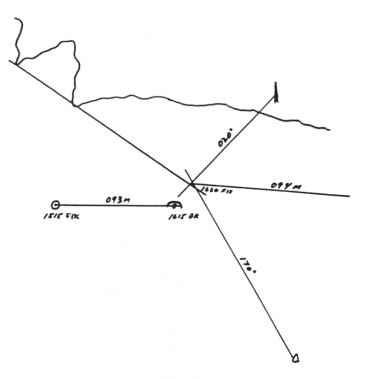

Figure 26

compare it to the depth shown on the chart for that location. This can confirm the accuracy of the fix. Use the fathometer for all DR plots also.

As you continue along the coast, there's a point of land ahead with some rocks off of it. You want to be sure to be far enough off the point to avoid them. There are various ways of accomplishing this. One is to use a sextant on the object and consult tables that tell you your distance off. Another is to use a range finder. However you must know the height of the object which isn't a problem with a navigational light since their height is usually written on the chart or is at least listed in the government printed light list. Then describe an arc with a compass (as in Figure 27) that encompasses all the rocks or hazards. Let's say it's half a mile in this case. Mark it down as a danger range of .05NM (nautical miles) and make sure that your range-finder readings keep you outside this distance off the object.

Since a small sailboat may not have the necessary instruments aboard, there are other ways to stay clear of the rocks. Keep careful track of your course and speed. Plot a bearing on the landmark as the lighthouse in Figure 27. If you know you're sailing six knots and it's been five minutes between the two bearings, you will have sailed half a mile. After five minutes of sailing, take and plot a second bearing. Place your dividers so the points are half a mile apart. Set your parallel

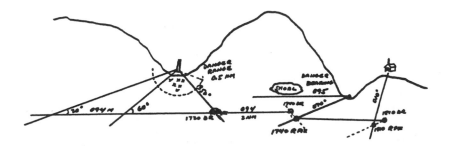

Figure 27

rulers on the compass course of your boat's heading and run them across the two bearings until the dividers show the bearings to be half a mile apart. Then draw your course line and see if you clear the rocks. Remember that an adverse current means you won't have sailed half a mile in the five minutes and you could very well be closer to shore than you estimate. In a fair current the opposite is true.

Figure 27 shows a method sometimes used to determine distance off an object. A bearing is taken relative to the bow of the boat (called a "relative bearing"). Let's say it's 30°. When that bearing becomes double, 60°, the distance you have sailed between the two sightings equals the distance to the object from your boat when you took the second bearing. It's called "doubling the angle." Another is called "bow and beam" bearings. Take a bearing when the object is 45° off the bow of the boat. When the object is abeam, 90° from the boat, the distance run from the time of taking the first bearing equals the distance to the object when it's abeam.

Continuing on the trip along the shore in Figure 27, you have taken a DR position at 1720 after sailing an hour from the previous fix. You have combined it with a bearing on the lighthouse of 350M, but it's not a fix because it's only one LOP, not two or more. You know there's a shoal that you must stay seaward of so you draw a line on the chart from the light on the next point that just clears the shoal. This line turns out to be 095M and is called the "danger bearing." Any bearing we subsequently take of the light that is 094M or lower keeps you clear of the shoal. If you take a bearing and it's 096M or higher, you are inshore of the 095 danger bearing and could possibly hit the shoal.

You are still sailing six knots and twenty minutes later at 1740 you take a bearing on the light and find it bears 070M. You know you have sailed a course of 094M and have sailed two nautical miles in twenty minutes. Your DR doesn't cross with the new bearing. Advance your first bearing two miles so it runs through the 1740 DR and is parallel (350°) to the first bearing (the dotted line). Where it intersects your bearing on the second object is called a "running fix." Mark it "1740 R Fix" and continue your 094 heading from that new fix. Half an hour (three nautical miles) later at 1810 you take a bearing on a church ashore and fine it to be 010M. Your 1810 DR again doesn't coincide with the bearing. Advance your second bearing (070M) three miles to the 1810 DR (the dotted lines) and the point it crosses the bearing on the church is your 1810 running fix.

CURRENT

Current comes with tidal depth changes, and is quite a large factor in navigation as the current velocity becomes a large percentage of the boat's speed. Therefore, it's particularly a factor in sailing. A sailboat averaging 5 knots may be sailing in a current 20% to 40% (1 to 2 knots) of its speed.

The tidal Current Tables printed by the U.S. Government give the maximum flood and ebb current and the time when the current changes direction. Tidal Current Charts are printed for twelve bodies of water on the east and west coasts, and are very handy in navigating and planning a cruise. These two are combined in a publication called the Eldridge Tide and Pilot Book, which covers the northeast coast. Photo 51 shows a page from the current tables and several of the charts (approximately one for each hour of the tide).

Assume it is now 1200 hours on August 20th. The tide tables indicate that water started flooding (coming into) Long Island Sound at the Race (a narrow passage between the mainland and the tip of Long Island) at 0914 hours (see the underlined numbers in Photo 51). We must add an hour for Daylight Saving Time, so we get 1014 hours. It is now about two hours after the current started flooding at the Race, so the top chart is the appropriate one in the photograph. Let's say we locate our present position on the chart and find that the current is 0.5 knots in a direction of about 265° True.

Photo 52

Determine the course to steer in a given current.

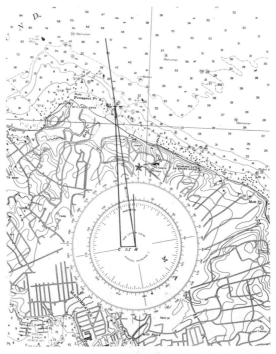

Figure 28

Draw course of 001M. Draw current at 265T. Swing 5NM line CE to intersect desired course. Parallel line (007M) is course to steer.

We transfer this information to a chart, as in Photo 52. We are sailing from A to B on a course of 001°M. First we draw line AC one-half mile long, indicating the effect of the current on the boat in one hour. Next we take the boat speed (5 knots in this case) and describe arc D to intersect course line AB at point E. Line CE will be the course to steer (007°M), and A to E will be our progress toward our destination in one hour. If the current velocity or direction changes over the period of time it takes us to reach our destination, we can use an average current for our calculations.

Rather than transfer these courses all over to our position on the chart, the same course to steer can be determined by drawing the current diagram right on the compass rose in the same manner. Figure 28 shows how it's done.

When your DR includes allowances for current and leeway most navigators call it an "estimated position" and mark it "EP" on the chart with the time. Some navigators even draw two separate plots, one DR and one EP until a fix can be obtained.

There are some other aspects of navigation that can be helpful. All charts show the topography of the land masses. The height and steepness of the hills are shown by numbers and topographical contours.

Until I started to look closely at these on a chart, every piece of shoreline looked like every other. When the contour lines are close together, indicating a steep slope, it's quite often easy to spot the hill it represents. The heights of the peaks are usually marked on the chart. Of two nearby summits, one may be 400 feet high and other 600 feet high. When you look at the shore, the perspective of the two summits to another can give you a good idea of your geographical relationship to them.

Another secret to safe navigation is to be very skeptical of your work. Once a fix is plotted, check it by looking around to see if it makes sense. According to your position, do nearby objects appear in the proper perspective? Is that island really on your starboard bow as your fix shows? This is the type of reasoning you follow to check yourself.

Nothing beats reading the number right off a buoy if it's close enough in order to verify that it's the right one. Once you've navigated awhile in fog, low visibility, and current, buoys that seem to confirm your position often turn out to be the wrong ones on closer inspection. If you don't check the number or otherwise confirm your position, you might make a course alteration on the assumption that your navigation is correct and really end up in trouble. If you aren't sure, quickly plot a second fix to check the first, and so on. With practice you will gain confidence in your work and will more easily be able to catch mistakes before they can cause danger.

POLAR DIAGRAMS

To get the best performance out of your sailboat, you should have a basic understanding of VMG (velocity made good) and polar diagrams.

We know that sailboats on different points of sailing sail at different speeds in the same wind strength. A boat sailing upwind usually sails slower than a boat on a reach. If we're sailing to a destination upwind, the boat with the best VMG, speed directly upwind, will get there first. Look at figure 29. Boat A has dropped out of the race, turned on their engine and is powering directly upwind at five knots. Their VMG is five knots. Boat B is continuing to race and is closehauled at 45° to the wind direction and is also sailing at five knots. If we draw a line over to Boat B's course perpendicular to the wind direction, we see that boat B is sailing only 3.3 knots directly upwind. Boat C's skipper says, "I can sail faster than boat B if I sail about 15° lower" and gets the boat up to 6 knots by sailing lower. But the result, when you draw the perpendicular line, is boat C is sailing only 2.7 knots upwind.

The same works for boats sailing downwind. Boat E is sailing very fast on a broad reach, but her VMG to leeward is only 3.2 knots. Boat F is sailing 1.5

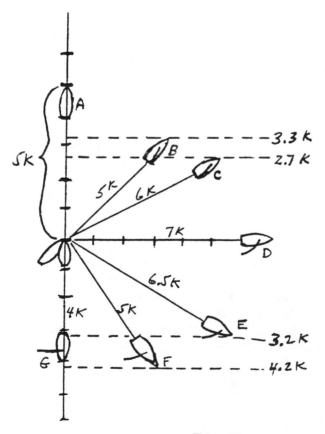

Figure 29

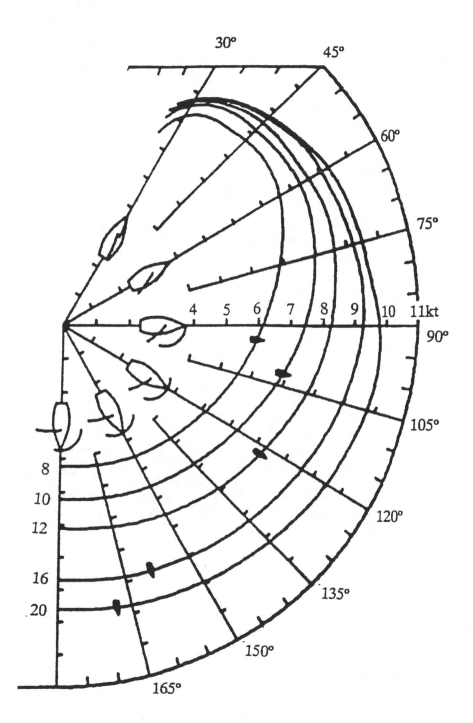

Figure 30

knots slower, but her VMG to leeward is almost a knot faster. Boat G is sailing directly downwind, but only at 4 knots, because it's a slow point of sailing.

If we connect the bows of these hypothetical boats, we get a curve which is the position of each boat in 10 knots of wind depending on the angle to the wind they're sailing. This is a polar diagram.

Normally, a polar will show curves depicting boatspeed at various wind strengths for a particular boat. In Fig. 30 the wind strength curves are at 8, 10, 12, 16 & 20 knots and show the optimum speeds for a 54' sailboat both beating and running. The solid boats depict the optimum run angles as taken from the table below.

BOAT SPEED AS A FUNCTION OF TRUE WIND VELOCITY AND APPARENT WIND ANGLE:

WIND	OPTIMUM VMG BEAT	OPTIMUM VMG RUN	OPTIMUM RUN ANGLE
8kt	4.415	4.753	94°
10kt	5.015	5.707	102°
12kt	5.397	6.471	122°
16kt	5.800	7.774	159°
20kt	5.970	8.657	168°

The curves are calculated on either true wind angle or apparent wind angle. Since the apparent wind is that which we feel and see on the boat as it sails, the apparent wind angle is easiest to work with in polars. For instance, the polar diagram shows the best downwind VMG for 10 knots of breeze is at 102° apparent wind angle. Just sail the boat so the apparent wind is 102°. This is taken directly from your apparent wind indicator or "AWI". If you don't have wind instruments, judge the angle from your masthead fly.

To obtain a performance package for your boat, just call US SAILING, the governing body of sailing at 401-849-5200 or write them at PO Box 209, Newport, RI 02840.

TEST QUESTIONS ON CHAPTER IV

1. Is a "large scale" chart of a small geographical area or a large one?
2. What is the nautical distance in one minute of latitude?
3. What percentage of the total tide rise and fall occurs in the first two hours of a six hour tide?
4. What is the acronym we use for compass errors?
5. What is a "danger bearing?"
6. What bearing does not require a compass?
7. What is "Doubling the Angle?"
8. What is a "running fix?"
9. What does "DR" and "EP" stand for?
10. What do contour lines on a chart show you?

ANSWERS

1. A small area.
2. One nautical mile.
3. 25%.
4. CADET.
5. A bearing on an object that keeps you clear of a hazard.
6. The lining up of two points of land.
7. A method of determining distance from an object. The distance traveled from the 1st bearing to the 2nd bearing is the same as from the 2nd bearing to the object.
8. A fix obtained by crossing a present bearing with a past bearing which has been advanced the distance traveled between bearings.
9. Dead Reckoning and Estimated Position.
10. The steepness and height of the terrain.

CHAPTER V

SAFETY AND EMERGENCIES:

OBSERVING WEAKNESSES

Safety is both the prevention of emergencies and the preparation for them, when and if they occur. It may take years of experience, but some people are able to develop a sixth sense of when something is not quite right. For instance, I went for a one hour sail to check out some new jibs for our 54' ocean racer SLEUTH. It was my first sail in six months, yet I noticed that someone had shackled on one of the mainsheet blocks a quarter turn from lining up properly with the sheet pull. If it had been blowing harder and we had trimmed the sheet in tightly, we would have twisted, weakened and possibly broken the bale on which the block was attached. We immediately corrected it and not five minutes later I noticed someone had used a bolt with a non-locking nut on our starboard running backstay. If the nut came off and the bolt popped out we could have lost the mast. Neither of these examples seem like anything worth bothering about on a boat and an untrained eye would miss them completely. But knowing what the end result may be if they are not corrected comes from long experience and training.

In fact, some sailors never seem to be able to develop this sixth sense although much of it is no mystery. You've seen something break before and you look out for it. A few years ago I advised an Olympic contender that he'd better change his spinnaker halyard shackle before competing in the final races. Sure enough, it broke the next day in a practice race. I just happened to know it was a weak design.

I could give you hundreds of examples that have happened to me, but I doubt that would help the reader because each boat and event is a little different. Suffice it to say many emergencies can be avoided by being observant. Here are some of the things to look for:

1. Corrosion or hairline splits in shroud swage fittings that attach to the turnbuckles.

2. A broken strand in a shroud or stay.

3. Evidence of chafe on rope halyards, burrs on wire halyards.

4. Excessive water in the bilge, corrosion around thru-hull fittings.

5. A captive pin halyard shackle that needs spreading to keep the pin from flopping around.

6. Lack of seizing wire on anchor shackles.

7. Sharp untaped cotter pins that can rip sails.

8. Sharp edges on the boom that can also rip sails.

9. Loose or funny-feeling steering.

10. Loose shackle pins on important items like hiking straps. If they let go, you can end up overboard.

11. No cotter pins in shroud turnbuckles (often forgotten by the person tuning the rig, with possible loss of the mast resulting).

12. Note loss of cotter pins from any clevis pins you see.

13. Signs of weakness in the area of the main boom gooseneck. This is an area of tremendous strains and can be dangerous if the boom breaks free.

14. Make sure that the covers for any "water-tight" compartments are securely fastened in case the cockpit fills with water.

15. Any loose deck blocks, travelers or winches indicate that the nuts on some of the through-bolts have backed off. Any undue strain on the block might cause it to pop off the deck.

16. A bad lead on an anchor line or mooring line may cause chafe and the loss of your boat hours after you've left it for the night.

17. Broken stitching in a batten pocket. Small tears in a sail.

Most of the above are found on small boats. With cruising boats there are a myriad of other things that can go wrong because we're introducing far greater strains, engine and electrical problems, dinghy and propeller tangling problems, among many others.

The old adage "an ounce of prevention is worth a pound of cure" is especially apropos on a boat. So before you go out, try to spot the various potential sources of eventual emergencies and correct them.

HANDLING EMERGENCIES

Let's imagine that you have not noticed the signs of trouble before going out sailing for the day. Certain emergencies occur. How do you handle them?

The first situation occurs because you didn't notice the cracks in the swaged fitting on your starboard upper shroud. It breaks when you are on a starboard tack and the mast bends perilously to leeward. Immediately spin the boat into the wind dumping air out of the mainsail and jib and flipping over to the port tack. This puts the pressure on the unbroken port shrouds and saves the mast. If you can't go on port tack for some reason such as proximity to shore, shoot into the wind, get your sails down and anchor. If a wire shroud breaks and the break is near the turnbuckle and you have some U-bolts aboard, you can make another eye and reattach the turnbuckle assuming it's a small sailboat. Or you can take both ends of the spinnaker halyard out to the edge of the deck and fasten it securely. If it's a double-ended halyard and one end is still attached to the mast, stretch can cause poor support, so attach both ends to the deck edge. If possible, shinny up the mast and pull the halyard out to the spreader tip with a looped line so the spreader can help support the mast as it does with the upper shroud.

Occasionally the backstay breaks on a sailboat. If it happens when running downwind, the mast could fall forward over the bow because of the pull of the spinnaker and the mainsail. The first thing to do if it breaks is to throw off the spinnaker sheet and round up into the wind immediately. Get the spinnaker down and luff the mainsail and jib immediately. This takes the pressure off the sails and wind resistance pushes the mast and rigging towards the stern of the boat. Then trim in the mainsail tight. The leech of the mainsail on a small boat will almost have the same holding power as the backstay. Note the number of parts on the main sheet and the strength with which you haul it in. Make sure the traveler is centered in the middle of the boat for maximum mast support. In moderate winds you can sail on most points of sail with the main trimmed in as if close-hauled. In heavier winds the main can be reefed down quite far and still give some support and allow you to sail to a destination. However, the support will only be to the point where the head of the sail is on the mast. To support the upper part of the mast secure the spinnaker halyard aft at the stern on boats where the spinnaker halyard runs to the top of the mast.

Another option in heavy winds is to douse the mainsail and run the main halyard either to the end of the boom or to the stern. By attaching the main halyard to the end of the boom, cleating the other end and trimming the mainsheet tightly we get excellent mast support. Attach the halyard to a boom bale, not the outhaul, because the latter can break. On larger sailboats with a main halyard winch, we would shackle the halyard right to the stern of the boat (or to an extra line if the halyard wasn't long enough) and tension it tightly by use of the winch.

Usually when a jibstay breaks the crew has a little time before the mast falls backwards because the jib luff will support it for awhile. The proper maneuver is to head downwind and ease the mainsail immediately. The force of the wind in the mainsail will push the mast forward and keep it standing. It's also fairly easy to find another unused halyard, (either spinnaker or spare jib halyard on many boats) to attach to the bow for temporary support. When you get into the harbor, lower the mainsail first and then take care of the jib.

Sometimes the windward spreader breaks. The same procedures apply as when a shroud breaks. Tack or jibe immediately to put the strain on the good spreader on the other side of the mast. If you can sail on that tack back to the harbor you don't have to worry about repairing the spreader. More often, though, you have to make repairs in order to be able to sail on the initial tack with the broken spreader. Search around the boat for a piece of wood or tubing with which to splint the spreader. On a Soling and other small boats, remember there's the tiller extension, deck supports, floorboard supports and other things that might be used. If you're desperate, even the tiller could be used. Then steer with the sails and a pair of pliers or vice grips attached to the rudder head. The key to survival in any situation is to be as inventive as possible.

In the case of a lost rudder, there is no way to replace it. On a larger boat there are usually tools available to attach a floorboard to one end of the spinnaker pole and the other end to the transom therby creating a sweep oar for steering, but even this is not as effective as the method taught in Offshore Sailing School's Learn to Sail course — steering the boat with the sails alone. To review: Just trim and cleat the jib. Then play the mainsail, easing it to head off and trimming it to head up. Put crew weight to windward to head off, to leeward to head up. To tack, free the jib and trim the main. Then, when head to wind, back the jib to make sure the bow gets completely across the eye of the wind. Jibing can only be done in light winds: ease the mainsail out completely and back the jib to windward to force the bow down to a run. Then get all the crew weight way out over the windward side to increase lee helm. The main should swing over to the other jibe, but don't trim it in after it does because the boat will round right up in a broach.

Sinking is not a common emergency, thank God, but it can happen that the boat fills up with water to the extent that sinking is a possibility. If a small boat broaches on a spinnaker run and a crew releases the spinnaker guy, the spinnaker may lay the boat over flat and it's likely the cockpit will fill with water. With the forward and aft hatches closed there should be no problem. Get the spinnaker down and luff the sails so the boat straightens up. Then bail like crazy with buckets. I like to have at least one bucket on any boat I sail. A cruising boat should have many. Pumps do a good job but they are unreliable as debris can clog the intake. Moreover, only one crew member can usually pump whereas many can bail with buckets.

While sailing with the boat full of water, head for shallow water so the boat will be easily recoverable if it sinks. Under no circumstances should you make any violent alteration of course. I once saw a boat that was full of water sailing on a reach towards the shore. The helmsman decided to round up into the wind and stop the boat in order to bail more efficiently. The boat turned, but the water in the boat kept on going in the original direction of travel. The weight and force of the water rolled the boat flat over. It filled the rest of the way and sank.

In such conditions the crew should already have lifevests on. When it's obvious that there's nothing that can be done to avoid sinking, try to tie a fender or some floating item to a long line such as a spinnaker sheet to mark the location of the boat for salvage later. You'd be surprised how much time you actually have. Air is usually trapped under the deck and the last throes are really quite slow as the bow or stern finally disappears beneath the waves. Make sure that the crew is well clear of the boat and in no way entangled in the various lines as she sinks.

Many daysailers have forward and aft compartments. As long as they are tight the boat will float. However, a collision with another boat can result in a hole in one of the compartments. During one of our racing courses such a collision occurred puncturing the aft compartment of a Soling. On one tack the hole was submerged, on the other it was out of the water. The obvious procedure is to stay on the tack which keeps the hole out of the water until temporary repairs can be made. This particular crew didn't do that. Then one of the crew members opened up the aft compartment hatch to see if he could plug the hole from the inside. The effort was well-intentioned, but misguided. Water poured into the cockpit from the compartment and the crew barely got the hatch refastened. If the cockpit had also filled with water the Soling couldn't have remained afloat.

There are a few things that can be done about a hole under the waterline in a boat. First stuff clothes or blankets in the hole. Next cover it from the outside with plastic and then cover the plastic with a blanket or sails fixed in place with lines that go right under the boat and tie to either side. I have never had to resort to this and I hope I never will. The water pressure is said to hold the collision mat in place, but I'll believe it's a practical solution when I've had to try it. Nevertheless, it doesn't hurt to have some kind of solution in mind for emergencies that have never happened to you.

SQUALLS

Squalls are small, local, generally unforecast storms. They often form on hot summer days as a result of nearby land heating up. This causes the air to rise and large cumulus clouds to form. These thunderheads are often anvil shaped and quite dark down low. There may be almost no wind as a squall approaches and suddenly you're met by a strong blast coming out of it. Then, as it passes, the wind will shift — often as much as 180°.

Other types of squalls are associated with frontal passages and can be fairly accurately forecast. If the weather forecast has predicted a front to pass, you may expect some prefrontal squalls in the neighborhood.

Judging Intensity

The problem for sailors is to determine beforehand just how intense the squall will be. Quite often the experience you have had from past squalls in a given location will suggest what to expect for future ones. For instance, when a nasty looking squall hit us once or twice a winter in the Bahamas it was as bad as it looked: blowing sixty with a driving rain. In the Virgin Islands, a squall that looked exactly the same as it approached rarely had over 35 knot winds. The result is one views a squall with a great deal more caution in the Bahamas than in the Virgins. Yet nothing is absolute and many squalls have the potential of great damage. Near Captiva Island, Florida a squall's intensity can be deceiving. We were hit by one squall a few winters ago that developed into a twister five miles after it passed us, knocking over house trailers on nearby Pine Island.

It's best to treat any approaching squall with respect. Try to look for signs that might measure its force and don't be fooled too much by darkness. On a bright sunny day a low bank of clouds in the distance casts a shadow underneath that looks very ominous. Yet when the bank arrives, there's nothing there except a solid blanket of low lying clouds instead of the sun you had previously. Had you shortened sail because of it, you'd have felt very foolish. Without any vertical development of the clouds, there's not apt to be much increase in wind velocity.

The squalls I get concerned about are those that stand out as very dark on an already overcast day which means the cloud layer is very thick right down close to the water surface. Often there's a pink tinge underneath which I can't account for, but when you see the pink tinge — watch out! It's apt to be a dilly. Obvious white caps in the distance also warn you of a high intensity squall. If you're lucky enough to have other boats between you and the squall, watch how the winds affect them. If you see them knocked flat by the squall, quickly shorten or douse sail yourself. If they just disappear into the darkness of the squall without appearing to be affected by it, don't be lulled into believing the squall has no power. After the boats disappear from your sight it's possible they might be hit by a blast. However, if there's no strong wind visible on initial entry into the squall there's not apt to be much wind further into it.

Preparation

In Solings and other small keelboats, the proper way to prepare for a squall is to first make sure that the flotation compartments are fastened securely closed. All crew should put on flotation vests, then get the anchor out and coil the line properly so it can run freely.

Take the bitter end of the line and run it through the bow eye and aft to the mast. Wrap the line twice around the mast and tie a bowline. Now overhaul the line through the bow eye and coil it neatly in the cockpit. Do this before the squall hits, because getting up on the foredeck in the middle of the squall could be very dangerous. If you slipped overboard there's no way the crew could come back to pick you up if the squall was an extremely violent one. Anchoring from the cockpit in the middle of a squall, without leading the line to the bow, will cause great complications. The boat will be broadside to the seas which will put a great strain on the anchor, the line and the point of attachment to the boat.

Something will have to give. If it holds for a while, the waves will smash against the side of the boat and fill up the cockpit.

If you are certain you can sail back into the harbor before the squall hits that's the best solution to the squall management problem. Don't attempt it if you are not certain. Nothing's worse than being hit by the squall in an area of restricted mobility surrounded by shoals. Its far better to get away from shallow water, even if it means heading away from the harbor, if you can't get safely inside before it hits.

Dousing Sails

The first sail to lower is the largest one. On most small boats it's the mainsail. When the first blast hits, the mainsail will lay you over (if it hasn't been doused) and easing the mainsheet doesn't help much. The boom hits the water because of the heeling of the boat and pushes it in just when you want to ease it more. With the mainsail unable to be eased the heeling increases and eventually the boat will swamp — the cockpit will fill with water.

So get the mainsail down. Assign emergency positions so each person knows their specific task: releasing the mainsheet, boom vang and cunningham, or unhooking the halyard while holding the boom up to free the leech. Remember that all tasks are much more difficult to perform when it's very windy so allow a little extra time. Be sure to take the halyard off the mainsail so it can't accidently fly out like a spinnaker attached only by the head and foot. Then flake the mainsail on the boom as neatly as possible, wrap the head around all the flakes once or twice and tie the whole sail snugly with the mainsheet.

With only the jib up in heavy winds you will be able to sail as high as a beam reach, but it is doubtful that you will be able to make any headway to windward. The stronger the wind becomes, the more you will have to run before it. If running before it at high speed is not getting you anywhere advantageous, you will probably want to reduce speed by dousing the jib and running "under bare poles." Lower the jib and keep both jib sheets tight as the sail comes down so the clew is centered right in front of the mast and the foot is stretched taut. Reach forward and tuck the body of the sail under the foot to avoid having much of the sail go over the side. If possibly try to wrap the spinnaker pole foreguy or the ends of the jib sheets around the sail to furl it. Don't go up on the foredeck. Stay in the cockpit and if you can't get the jib neatly rolled up and secured, don't worry about it. As long as the foot is tight and the sail is well lowered, you won't have too much trouble.

If you're still traveling too fast on a larger boat than a Soling or if you're in water too deep to anchor, consider dragging a warp or sea anchor off the stern. A warp is just a towline without the tow. Resistance can be added to it by attaching sailbags or a bucket or by just adding more line thus making it longer.

Anchoring

All this is fine where there's plenty of sea room, but in the presence of land or shoals, movement over the bottom must be reduced or stopped. This is where our anchoring preparations come in. Double check that the anchorlines won't wrap around anything such as someone's leg as it runs out. With a good head of speed, round up into the wind and lower the anchor over the side. Since you have overhauled the line aft of the bow eye, you can wrap it around the jib sheet winch and pay it out. This should be done relatively smartly. Using the jib winch allows you to increase the scope more slowly after the anchor has a good bite. It avoids the possibility of breaking the line which could happen if you tossed all the line overboard and waited for the anchor to bite and the boat to reach the end of the line with one gigantic jerk. Remember there are presumably heavy seas running and the boat could be surging down one of these seas when the end of the line was reached. Moreover, paying the line out under control keeps the bow headed into the seas, thereby offering less resistance to the waves. And lastly, the chance of someone or something getting caught in the line zinging out is diminished.

Now that you are anchored and the anchorline is running over the foredeck, tuck the jib under it to curtail any flapping of the jib in the wind. Both now, and particularly when underway, keep the boat as dry as possible. Water in the boat makes the boat sluggish to handle and lowers the freeboard. Waves are able to come over the side more easily the lower she gets and soon you won't be able to keep up with the waves.

Heaving-to

Heaving-to is a handy thing to know about and practice, whether you want to stop sailing for a while and relax for lunch or some other activity, or you're caught in a violent storm. Trim in the mainsail tight and cleat it. Back the jib to the windward side and cleat it. Since the mainsail will be forcing the boat forward and up into the wind and the jib will be forcing the boat backwards and the bow down away from the wind, an equilibrium can be maintained. The tiller can be tied in the position that best augments the equilibrium—usually to leeward. The boat will move very slowly through the water making quite a bit of leeway depending on the wind strength.

A friend of mine has sailed thousands of miles with just his wife on a keel/centerboard cruising boat. When a storm hits he reefs the main, heaves-to and raises the centerboard. The boat makes such rapid leeway that it leaves a flat "wake" to windward that seems to level oncoming breaking waves. He and his wife then go below and play cards for a day or two until the storm passes, enjoying relative comfort without being tossed around by the seas.

GROUNDINGS

Sooner or later anyone who sails will go aground. Though often embarrassing, generally it's not dangerous unless it's the windward side of a reef. More often the bottom is sand or mud in a bay or sound and you've hit because you were sailing too close to shore in order to get out of the current, a sand bar shifted from its position on the chart or you weren't following your course on the chart closely enough. With a centerboard boat it's easy. Once you bump, raise the centerboard and head for deeper water.

A daysailer with a keel is a bit more difficult. The most important reaction when you first hit is to heel the boat immediately. Trim in the sails flat and get all your crew weight to leeward. More acrobatic crew members can walk out on the boom, as it's eased out over the water, leaning against the windward side of the mainsail. Others can hang on the leeward shrouds. Try to sway the boat by leaning in and then way out. By getting the boat to roll, the swing to leeward will be further than by weight alone.

If this doesn't work use the spinnaker pole to push off. This method is good if the bottom is hard, but with a muddy bottom, the pole just sinks into the mud. Plus it fouls up the jaws and springs in the pole with dried mud, rendering them useless for their designed purpose at a later time.

Another answer is to bite the bullet and get wet. A Soling draws 4'3". If you're hard aground the water is only about three feet deep. Get over the side and start shoving. Try to rotate the boat by pushing the bow from one side while someone else pushes the stern. For better purchase, take the anchor over the side and carry it out the full length of the anchor rode into deeper water. Even when the water gets deeper than your height, you can move the anchor out away from the boat. Rest the anchor on the bottom and with the line vertical lift and swim. Wear a life vest to increase your buoyancy and for safety. Be careful if there is a strong current that can carry you away from the boat. If the anchor isn't very heavy (and it's much lighter underwater) you should be able to move it. Back on the boat, wrap the anchorline around a jib sheet winch and crank. You can achieve tremendous pulling power in this manner and may very well pull the boat off. This is commonly called "kedging off."

Obviously another method is to accept some friendly assistance from a powerboat. I would suggest that you determine beforehand if there will be a charge and, if so, how much it will be. Some "helpful" people try to charge for their services afterwards. Use your own line rather than accepting one from the powerboat. I understand that, under Admiralty Law, salvage can be more readily claimed and hold up in court if you accept a tow line from the towboat rather than tossing yours.

When a couple of powerboats are helping, it's sometimes practical to have one pull on a halyard to heel the boat over further while the other pulls on the hull. Do NOT do this with a SOLING. We have lost two masts, because well-meaning rescuers pulled on the main halyard (after the mainsail was doused). The Soling mast is completely unsupported above the upper shrouds except for the backstay. Any side pull on the main halyard will break the upper part off. Also some masts on smaller boats, regardless of how strongly supported by stays, can't take the unusual force and direction of a powerboat pulling it over. Use this method only on a cruising boat.

DISTRESS SIGNALS

Most of us are aware of the normal distress signals such as the "SOS" signal ("Save our Ship"): •••----••• in Morse Code. However there are many other official distress signals listed in the International Rules of the Road:

a. A gun or other explosive signal fired at intervals of about a minute.

b. A continuous sounding with any fog-signalling apparatus.

c. Rockets or shells, throwing red stars fired one at a time at short intervals.

d. A signal sent by radio-telephone consisting of the spoken word "MAYDAY." This comes from the French "m'aider" meaning "help me." "MAYDAY" is only used when you are in grave and immediate danger to person or property. If not in distress, use the "urgent" signal "PAN" repeated three times. Don't forget to radio your position.

e. The International Code Signal of distress indicated by NC.

f. A signal consisting of a square flag having above or below it a ball or anything resembling a ball.

g. Flames on the vessel (as from a burning tar barrel, oil barrel, etc.).

h. A rocket parachute flare or a hand flare showing a red light.

i. A smoke signal giving off orange colored smoke.

j. Slowly and repeatedly raising and lowering arms outstretched each side.

k. The radio telegraph alarm signal.

l. The radio-telephone alarm signal.

m. Signals transmitted by emergency position-indicating radio beacon (commonly known as EPIRB).

I used to believe that an upside-down ensign or flag was a signal of distress but it's not on the official list.

Of the above, on a Soling we could use a flashlight S.O.S., the fog horn, possibly an ersatz flag and ball, a hand flare, a smoke signal and outstretched arms.

COLLISIONS

In Offshore Sailing School's Learn to Sail course, you learned the basic right of way rules. Let's briefly review them.

After many years of substantial differences, the Inland and International Rules of the Road are now, for all intents and purposes, identical. We have three possibilities: sail versus sail, sail versus power, and power versus power.

When you are sailing and meet another sailboat you are either 1) on opposite tacks, 2) on the same tack or 3) overtaking or being overtaken. On opposite tacks, the starboard tack boat has right of way. On the same tack, the leeward boat has right of way. In an overtaking situation, the overtaking boat must avoid hitting the overtaken boat.

When you are sailing and meet a boat under power, you have right of way in almost all cases. The few exceptions are when the motorboat is anchored or not under command, is fishing, is being overtaken by the sailboat or when the motorboat is a large vessel restricted in her ability to maneuver.

When you are under power and meet another powerboat, the one in the other's "danger zone" has right of way. The danger zone is the area from dead ahead to two points (22.5°) abaft the starboard beam. Any sailing vessel has to stay out of the way of a commercial vessel in a narrow channel when the latter can safely maneuver only in that channel.

In all the above cases, the boat with the right of way is the "stand-on" vessel. The boat that has to avoid the collision is the "give-way" vessel. The stand-on vessel must maintain her course and speed to avoid misleading the vessel giving way, but must, nevertheless, avoid a collision when it appears the give-way vessel is unable to fulfill her obligations to keep clear.

The important part, no matter which boat you are, is to determine very early if the chance of a collision exists. In the Learn to Sail course you learned that a collision will occur if the bearing between the two boats doesn't change. If we maintain a steady, constant course and line up something such as a shroud with the converging boat and the shroud continues to line up with the other boat minutes later, a collision can result. Or if we take a compass bearing, a more accurate method, and the bearing doesn't change as the boats get closer together, watch out for a potential collision. But let me recommend a very practical and simple method to achieve the same thing. The only requirement to use this system is that there be land a mile or so behind the other boat. As you converge with the other boat watch the relationship between the other boat and the land. If the other boat appears to be moving forward past the land, she will cross you. If the other boat appears to be losing ground on the land, you will cross her. But if she remains stationary against the land, you are on a collision course. The crew will generally watch the other boat and tell the skipper that he or she is gaining ("making land") or losing.

The biggest cause of collisions and near misses is inattentiveness. Sailors get notoriously lulled into a sense of solitude. Even in fairly crowded waters the sea gives a feeling of spaciousness. Sailboats travel very slowly compared to the high speed we're used to on the highways, so we don't have the same feeling of a need for alertness. Yet two boats a mile apart each sailing at six knots, can hit each other in five minutes. An all too common comment after a near miss is, "Where the devil did *he* come from?" The boat was always there, but just unnoticed. This is a very good reson why drinking and sailing don't mix. Save the drinking for after you're anchored and not expecting to go sailing again that day.

Night Collisions

It's not unusual for the breeze to die around dusk and sailors who have ventured too far away from home may find themselves caught out after sundown. Make sure, therefore, that your boat has all the necessary lights and emergency flares for night sailing. A small sailboat under 20 meters (roughly 65') must have red and green sidelights, but they may be combined on the centerline. There are a number of flashlight battery types on the market for small sailboats. A sternlight is also required and it's a good idea to have a fairly strong battery-powered spotlight aboard.

Probably the largest concern after dark is being run down by a commercial vessel such as a tugboat with a tow. Recently, in Long Island Sound, a motor yacht was struck by a barge being towed by a tug and five lives were lost. It behooves you to understand the lights on such tugs because the tows are often way far behind and weakly lit. If you mistakenly sail in front of the tow at night you're out of luck. The tow can't swerve to avoid you, nor can it stop on its own. It's even unlikely that there is anyone riding on the towed barge, so there's no one to see the accident and call for help. Plus the tug's crew, sometimes 300 yards (three football field lengths) ahead, is not apt to see or hear anything at night. It's crucial, therefore, to correctly establish whether there is a barge. The rule is simple. If the tow is more than 200 meters behind, the tug carries three 225° masthead white lights arranged vertically on a staff and a yellow towing light above the stern light. If the tow is less than 200 meters back, you will see two vertical lights and a yellow towing light. If the tow is alongside the tug, two vertical white lights are shown, but no yellow towing light. These are in addition to the normal side lights, and sternlight. Where there are no white lights arranged vertically, there is no tow and you can safely pass astern of the tug. There will be a masthead light forward and a higher one aft of it as in most other powerboats.

Let's say you see a boat on a collision course with the normal lights plus a green light over a white light vertically. This is a trawler dragging nets and has right of way over you. There are a number of other types of vessels with unusual lights you may encounter out at night and if you can't identify them, the safest procedure is to take compass bearings to determine if you're on a collision course. If you are, make a large alteration of course to stay away from them. There's a saying, "He was right, dead right, as he sailed along and now he's as dead as if he'd been wrong." Don't push your right of way, especially at night.

When it appears that there may be a close call developing, and the other vessel may not be aware of your existence, the spotlight mentioned previously can come in handy. The traditional method to display your presence has been to flash the light up on your sails to illuminate them for the vessel's skipper to see. I've found this works well on nights with a good visibility but is next to useless in bad conditions (when you most need to be seen). Shine the spotlight right at the wheelhouse of the vessel. From this vantage the battery-operated spot light will look like a pinprick of light, if they see it at all. It certainly won't blind the helmsman, which you obviously want to avoid, but will enable them to see that there's a boat out there they may not have been aware of.

Many people use binoculars during the day, but forget that a good set of binoculars can save a great deal of inner stress at dusk or at night. I was in a situation one time where we were converging with a number of commercial boats and it was hard to know exactly what they were doing. The lights seemed confusing. By checking with binoculars we found we could cross one tug towing a barge and sail between it and another tug towing a barge to windward of the first tug and tow. Until using binoculars we couldn't tell who was towing what. In another situation we were converging at dusk with a ship that was all lit up like a Christmas tree. We couldn't pick out the side lights and had no idea which way it was going. A check with binoculars showed it to be a large sailing schooner with a generator that accounted for all the lights and we easily set a course to avoid her.

TEST QUESTIONS ON CHAPTER V

1. If a shroud breaks, what is the first thing to do?
2. To steer without a rudder, how do you head off?
3. What can happen if you quickly turn a boat that's full of water?
4. What indicates an intense squall?
5. What do three vertical lights on a powerboat indicate to you?
6. Which sail is doused first in a squall?
7. What is a "warp?"
8. What is "kedging?"
9. What is the Morse Code distress signal?
10. What is the origin of the word "Mayday?"

ANSWERS

1. Flip over to the opposite tack.
2. Ease the mainsail and trim the jib.
3. The water will continue in a straight line and roll the boat over.
4. High vertical development, extremely dark underneath with a possible pink tinge, white caps, other boats in trouble.
5. A tow more than 200 meters behind.
6. The largest.
7. A line over the stern of the boat to slow it down.
8. Setting out an anchor to pull a grounded boat off a shoal area.
9. Three dots, three dashes and three dots. SOS for "Save Our Ship."
10. It comes from the French word "m'aider," meaning "help me."

The Complete Colgate
Sailing Library

Steve Colgate on Sailing by Steve Colgate. 416 pages of incomparable information. From basic terminology to cruising tips and racing, the most comprehensive book available. $29.95.

Colgate's Basic Sailing by Steve Colgate. Critics call it the best. Steve's style makes it easy. $9.95.

Performance Sailing by Steve Colgate. Seamanship, advanced sail trim, theory and navigation. $9.95

Fundamentals of Sailing, Cruising & Racing by Steve Colgate. 380 pages of sailing information published by W.W. Norton & Co. $24.95

Steve Colgate on Cruising by Steve Colgate. The complete guide to bareboat chartering. $12.95.

Manual of Racing Techniques by Steve Colgate. Excellent for new racers and preseason brush-up. $9.95.

Steve Colgate on the Racing Rules by Steve Colgate. A must for every racer. Each rule and definition is carefully analyzed in Steve's easy to read style. $10.95.

VIDEO TAPES
Learn to Sail Video Tape. 106 minutes of step by step basic-to-intermediate instruction with Steve Colgate and film stars Sam Jones and Audrey Landers. $29.95. VHS

Racing Rules Made Easy Video Tape. Understanding the rules has never been so easy. Hosted by Steve Colgate, each rule is explained in an easy-to-understand, streamlined manner. $39.95. VHS

ORDER TOLL FREE 800-221-4326

Or mail to: Offshore Sailing School
16731 McGregor Blvd.
Ft. Myers, FL   33908

NAME: (please print) _____

ADDRESS: _____

CITY: _____ STATE: _____ ZIP _____

HOME PHONE: _____ DAYTIME PHONE: _____

TITLE	PRICE
Shipping	
6% Sales Tax (Florida Residents Only)	
TOTAL	

Method of Payment: [ ] Check   [ ] Visa   [ ] Mastercard   [ ] Amex

Account Number: _____ Exp. Date _____

Signature: _____